ROOMS
TO GROW UP IN

Rosie Fisher

Salem

House

Salem House
Salem, New Hampshire

First published in the United States by
Salem House, 1985. A member of the
Merrimack Publishers' Circle, 47 Pelham Road,
Salem NH 03079.

ISBN 0-88162-084-X

Library of Congress Catalog Card Number 84-52465

This book was edited, designed and produced by
The Paul Press Ltd, 22 Bruton Street, London W1X 7DA

Art Editor Caroline Courtney
Senior Editor Jane Struthers
Designer Tony Paine
Assistant Editor Philippa Dyke
Illustrations Sally Launder
Plans Hayward and Martin Limited
Photography Jon Bouchier, Bruton Photography

Editorial Director Jeremy Harwood
Art Director Stephen McCurdy
Publishing Director Nigel Perryman

Cover mural by Anna de Polnay

Typeset by Wordsmiths, Street, Somerset
Origination by Tempus Litho Limited, London
Printed and bound in Italy

To my mother – in memory of unforgotten times

I would like to thank all those who have helped me put this book
together. Firstly, Jeremy Harwood, who encouraged me to write the
book, and also Steve McCurdy, Jane Struthers, Philippa Dyke and
Caroline Courtney for their artistic and literary guidance.
Special thanks to Stephen Hesmondhalgh for having agreed to
devise all the projects – not realizing quite what a project this was in
itself! To Trudi Nicholls for helping me so enthusiastically with all the
special effects pages. To all the other artists who contributed: Nessa
Kearney, Anna de Polnay, Claire Falcon, Cathy Stamp, Jane Maiden,
Penny Streeter, Valerie Schulz, Barbara Harrison, Sally Miles, Terry
Skinner, Hannerole Dehn, and Robert and Colleen Berry. To Dido
Farrell for taking over so competently in my absence. My special
thanks, too, to all the parents and children who allowed us to
photograph their rooms.
Finally, my thanks to Mark and my four children – Giles, Lucinda,
Rupert and Tara, who allowed me to shut myself away to write and
who put up with my bad temper when it wasn't going well!

FOREWORD

Dragons and all I hope that it stands for really just happened. I did not always have a burning desire to paint furniture for children and decorate their rooms – it was more a case of necessity being the mother of invention!

I am, at heart, an antiques dealer, and my shop in London started off on that basis, full of treasures from the past. Some of these were lovely old painted chairs, so, as a sideline, I had some new painted and decorated children's chairs created. These always walked out of the shop before anything else. This discovery coincided with the slump in the sale of traditional antiques and, with a bad-tempered bank manager on my hands, I had to think of something else to put in my shop that would sell a lot faster!

Being an ardent shopper and the mother of four children, I realized that there was a gap in the market. No one seemed to make furniture especially for children that was fun, yet classic in design. With the help of Bill Bilbe, we designed a table to go with the chairs and then a toy chest. When these looked right, I advertised in the local paper for artists to decorate the furniture. The telephone did not stop ringing! I was living in a hive of untapped artistic talent.

We got to work decorating the tables and toy chests and then proudly put them in the shop. Orders came flooding in! Slowly we added to the range, with shelves, a chest of drawers and so on – I can still remember how excited I was when we sold that first chest of drawers. People seemed to love what we were doing and their reaction inspired me to go on – to think up new ideas and new techniques for making furniture look attractive, yet practical, with many of the ideas coming from the customers themselves. Of course, we had our disasters, but slowly we learnt what people liked.

As our reputation grew, newspapers and magazines started to write about us, so soon I had wonderful artists literally knocking on my door asking for work. As a result, I was lucky enough to build up a team of really varied artists, without which Dragons would have been nothing. They helped me enormously, suggesting ideas and teaching me new techniques. It was truly great team work. We are now well-established – happily babies and children are not seasonal! So, hopefully, Dragons will continue to flourish.

Why am I giving away something of our secret in this book? Well, we are asked so many times how we do what we do – which paints to use, how to design a mural, how we drag furniture and so on – that I wanted to show that the ability to transform a child's room into paradise is within everyone's reach. I hope that dipping into *Rooms to grow up in* will encourage and help you to try this yourself.

Rosie Fisher 81

Rosie Fisher
London 1984

PRINCIPLES OF DESIGN

Every interior designer aims to get the best results out of a given space, using an instinctive understanding and feeling for colour, scale, light and textures. He or she is then able to blend these into a homogenous whole, creating a room which has a wonderful feel.

The most important point to remember is that a design scheme should reflect your tastes. Do not be hidebound by fashion, or by the decorative schemes of your friends. This is your chance to use your imagination to the full, and create a delightful, exciting room for your child to grow up in. Make the most of it!

Any room, however dingy, dark and uninspiring, can be transformed into something exciting with the help of a little imagination. Clever use of colour can alter the proportions of a room, making it seem larger or smaller, more inviting or more spacious, according to the shades you choose. A feeling for texture and pattern is also an intrinsic part of a good design. For example, a rich wall surface will demand a similar effect from the soft furnishings, adding warmth to a room.

Another very important part of good design is to know when to enhance your decor and when to leave features understated. Careful arrangement of the furniture or ornaments may lead the eye naturally to a point you wish to emphasize. For example, pretty borders at the top and bottom of a wall can focus the eye on a favourite painting. Other small touches, such as a well-placed, flourishing plant, or a collection of posters or friezes which are hung in interesting and logical groups, will also bring a room to life, and give it individuality.

The wave of pastel shades painted directly on to the floorboards of this room is an extremely effective device. The colours are taken from those used in the decorations, such as the cushions, chairs, tables, and even the yellow moon on the window sill, and link together the points of detail in the room.

ASSESSING A ROOM

Once you have decided to decorate a room specifically to suit your child or children, you will probably feel very excited and enthusiastic. However, before you begin work, you should know exactly where to start.

Firstly, take a long hard look at the potential the room offers. In the years to come, many of your child's memories will be centred around this room, so it is important to make it friendly, cosy, warm and imaginative. It also has to be somewhere in which he or she feels really at home and comfortable.

Assessing the room

Consider the size of the room first. Is it small, and do you want to make it look larger? Is it excessively large and unwelcoming? Are the proportions satisfactory? Are the windows small or large? Where does the sunlight fall? Does the room face north or south? Does it look or feel warm or cold? All these factors will influence your design and colour scheme.

Using colour effectively

Colour offers you almost unlimited scope as a designer. It can miraculously enlarge a room, or shrink one which seems massively over-sized.

If you find it hard to visualize a colour you think you might like, make a simple board, on which you can pin all the samples you have collected. If, for instance, you are undecided about your choice of wallpaper, paste a large sample of the paper you are considering on the board. The same applies to paint, when you could paint the possible colour on a large sheet of lining paper. Then hang up the paper in the room, with a snippet of the fabric you are considering for the curtains, and look at it at different times of the day and in different lights, both natural and artificial. If your choice still inspires you after a few days, you can confidently incorporate it into your design.

Choosing colour carefully

If the room is small and dark, decorate it in a softer, lighter colour; if it is large, opt for a bolder, more vibrant, tone. Colour can make or break your design. For instance, painting a small room in a strong red will make it seem even tinier. But if you choose a gentle pink or cream, the room will immediately appear much larger than it is in reality. There are strong cases for using both light and dark shades, too – it is well-known, for instance, that warm colours cheer up dark rooms with a poor source of natural light. Colours such as reds, oranges, magentas, emerald greens and yellows will seem to draw the walls in, whereas dark greens, blues, purples and greys will do the reverse.

If the room is very grand, and has many worthwhile architectural features, I am a firm believer in not using too much colour, as it can distract the eye from the other points you might wish to emphasize. Remember the secret of good design is knowing what to leave out, as well as what to include.

Making good first

Before you start work, you must make a thorough investigation of the room, to check it for structural problems. For example, if the floorboards are rotten, you will have to replace them before laying the flooring you have chosen. You may decide to varnish the bare floorboards, in which case now is the time to consider under-floor insulation, which will reduce draughts. Check the wiring, too. If it is faulty, it must be repaired before you begin work on the room.

Other considerations include the window frames, which should be in a good state of repair. You may find that they are rotting, in which case they should be replaced before the rot spreads to more frames. If your windows are operated by sash cords, you must check them for fraying, and replace any which are damaged. A broken sash cord is extremely dangerous, because the window will suddenly slam shut, and could badly hurt either you or your child. Make sure the

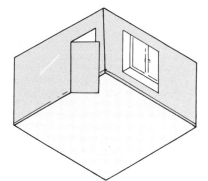

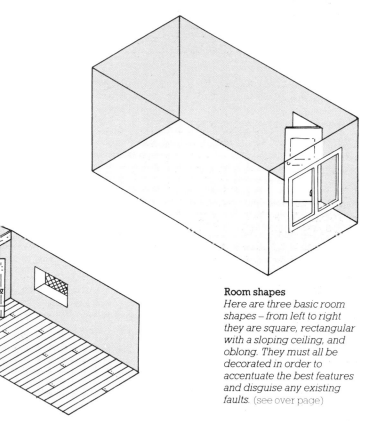

How to decorate
*Your choice of a decorative
scheme will be determined
by the existing features of
the room. The direction in
which a room faces, and the
amount of natural light it
receives will also be
important, and must be
taken into consideration.*

Room shapes
*Here are three basic room
shapes – from left to right
they are square, rectangular
with a sloping ceiling, and
oblong. They must all be
decorated in order to
accentuate the best features
and disguise any existing
faults.* (see over page)

skirting boards are sound, and fill any holes with proprietary wood filler.

You must also examine the walls and ceiling carefully for damp. This is not a condition which can be ignored, as it will only spread, and show through your new decoration. You must isolate the source of the damp, and treat it accordingly, consulting a professional if necessary.

Heating and lighting

You must consider heating – babies must be warm and snug – and lighting. If you have central heating, make sure the radiator never becomes hot enough to scorch, and locate any additional heaters above the child's reach, away from curious fingers.

Keep the lighting simple for a small child's room, when it is wisest to choose the much-maligned central light. You can use a child-proof nightlight in the evenings, if your child is frightened of the dark. Pretty table lamps are all

too easily knocked over once children begin to crawl and grab every table leg and electrical flex within reach. Give the light a striking shade to make it more attractive. Always design the room of a small child with safety in mind *(see pp24-5)*, and never sacrifice practicality for prettiness. You may regret it.

If your child is older, you will be able to experiment with different types of lighting. You can use side lights effectively, or highlight particular areas of the room with spotlights suspended from the ceiling and walls. In addition, dimmer switches will mean your child can alter the brightness of the lights, turning them up or down according to mood.

Finding the right flooring

Be careful to choose a suitable floor-covering, too, because children can be all too creative with plasticines, toothpaste, crayons and anything else that comes to hand! A thick pile carpet is

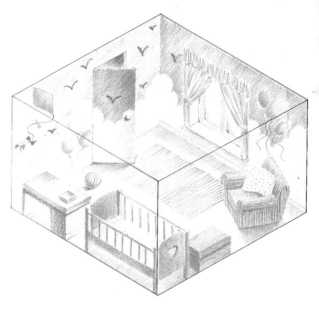

wonderfully extravagant and will look very impressive – but not for long. What's more, it will be a complete waste of money and time if you have to spend hours cleaning it!

A much more practical choice for small children's rooms is cork flooring, which looks warm and can be easily cleaned. You can always add a rug or two, fitted with non-slip strips, until your child is a little more house-trained, when you could fit a hard-wearing carpet, such as one made of cord.

If, like many houses, yours has wooden floor boards, you could make a feature of them, instead of covering them up. If so, you must make sure that the floor is even and the boards are splinter-free. One good idea is to cover the floor with several coats of paint, and then seal it with polyurethane. To make the room even more attractive, stencil a border of your own design around the edges of the floor.

Nursery
To liven up a basic box-shaped nursery, a mural has been painted on two of the walls, and extended over the door. The furniture has been pushed to the sides of the walls to give the baby enough room in which to crawl about. The rug on the carpet is non-slip to avoid accidents, and the curtains are heavy-duty so as to block out the light effectively.

Paint or paper?

Paint is an effective, and cheap, way of transforming even the most uninspiring room into something much more exciting. Wallpapering requires a higher degree of skill, but if you can master it, there are some very pretty papers on the market that are also good value.

You may find your choice dictated to a certain extent by the condition of the walls. Wallpapers are a better choice than paint if the surface of your walls is rather rough, as any minor defects will be hidden. Alternatively, you can fill in any holes in the walls, sand them down, and then cover them with lining paper, which will provide a smooth surface for a paint or wallpaper.

Creating a room to grow up in

If you are lucky enough to have a large room to decorate, it may be worth considering making it into a bedroom and playroom in one. In fact, why not give your child a real room to grow up in? This will provide a home for all those toys, and give your child somewhere to play. Remember that your aim is to create a room that your child can call his or her own. You may want to add a sofa-bed or bunk beds so your child can invite friends to stay overnight.

One of the most important points to bear in mind when designing your child's room is that children are naturally untidy and messy. You must therefore create the room accordingly. For example, if your child loves pillow fights, don't fill the room with small ornaments that could quickly be broken. Buy washable wallpapers and paints, and soft furnishings, which can be easily cleaned.

When very young, children need a lot of floor space, but as they get older they will need work tops and a comfortable chair or bean bag, so try to plan ahead whenever possible.

Painting a fantasy land

Have you ever wanted to fulfill the dream of creating a real fantasy land on the walls of your child's room? This is a wonderful opportunity to

Teenage room
The most important factor of a teenager's room is that it should provide workspace. This room has successfully combined practicality with an attractive design scheme. The desk has room for a computer, and the pinboard above it can be used both for decoration and for pinning up important study notes.

Before and after
The illustrations on these pages give design suggestions for the rooms pictured on the previous two pages.

Attic room
The existing features of wooden beams, a sloping ceiling and wooden floorboards have been used to create a country cottage feel in this room. Motifs have been stencilled above and below the beams, and extended around the room.

indulge your imagination to the full.

A mural is not as ambitious as it might sound – later I have shown you just how easy it can be to create one *(see pp60-1)*. You will have tremendous fun, too, planning the design with your child if he or she is old enough. Children who have grown up in a room designed just for them will always remember it with affection, especially if it contains their very own mural, perhaps featuring a favourite cartoon character.

Let your imagination flow

Designing a room for your child, or children, can be tremendously exciting, opening up new realms of imagination, whether you completely rebuild the room, or simply redecorate the walls and ceiling. Once you have assessed the potential and problem areas of the room you are to work on, you can let your imagination run riot. And this book will help you to enjoy the·experience to the utmost. Have fun!

USING FEATURES

If you are lucky, the room you plan to decorate will need little work on it. However, if you are faced with a more onerous decorating task, take heart, because very few problems are insurmountable.

Very often, your first reaction when assessing the fixtures and fittings of a room will be horror. You may believe that the room offers more problems than you can cope with, and decide that the only solution is to completely gut it and start from scratch. However, I firmly believe that you should not instantly rip out all the features you dislike. Given some thought, you can often camouflage the offending fixtures and even put them to good use.

Coping with cupboards

Ugly fitted cupboards can be real eyesores, especially if they have been cheaply made. However, there are many things which you can do to improve them. For example, you could paint them with a new base colour, and then cover them with some characters taken from your child's favourite book or cartoon. Trace them on, and then paint in the outlines, or stencil them on to the surface. A rabbit hopping here, a dragonfly floating there, or some flowers, leaves and bows are only a few of the possibilities you can use to enliven the dreariest cupboards.

Fitted cupboards can dominate a small room, if they are not camouflaged. By decorating them in the same manner as the rest of the room, using the same wallpaper or painting technique, they can blend into the background, and make the room look larger.

Accentuating alcoves

Make the most of any alcoves, and turn them into features, not flaws. An alcove can be the ideal place to install a hanging cupboard, or to fit a set of small bookshelves and build a fitted cupboard underneath. A simpler, and different, way of making use of an alcove is to fit a rail or shelves, and install a blind which pulls down to hide the inevitable clutter!

If the room has a tiny alcove set into a wall, even this can offer considerable designing scope. You could treat the alcove as a window, and paint in a scene, thus making a *trompe l'oeil (see pp92-3)*. Alternatively, if your child is an avid collector of something, such as shells or model aeroplanes, fit some shelves in the alcove, and use it as a display case.

Turning a problem into a feature

Try not to see sloping ceilings, wooden beams and irregularly-shaped rooms as potential problems. If incorporated into your design in an interesting way, they can add tremendous character to a room, and become an asset rather than a liability.

I am only too well aware, from practical experience, that these features in small, high-up bedrooms can cause initial problems. One of them is deciding where the walls end and the ceiling begins!

If this is a decision you have to make, it is far better to treat the ceiling and walls as one continuous surface. Paint the whole room in the same colour, or decorate it with the same wallpaper.

Managing a difficult ceiling

You can often disguise a problem by playing a trick on the eye. For example, if the ceiling seems intolerably low, you can make it appear higher by decorating it with a light colour. Equally, a ceiling which is too high will seem lower if it is painted or papered in a strong colour. Pay attention to the lighting, too, and set any overhead lights into low ceilings, rather than letting them hang downwards.

The sky's the limit

If the room you are designing has a very high ceiling, why waste the space? With careful planning, you may find that you can get twice the use out of one room. For example, you could build a small gallery at the top of the room, and use this area for the bed, or seating space. This will leave the floor as principally a play and work area for your child, and give you two rooms in one. Remember to think big!

Choosing the wallpaper

If you wish to wallpaper a room with a sloping ceiling, choose a design with a small pattern. Stripes, or a definite design, will cause problems, because you will find it virtually impossible to line up the pattern properly.

Remember, too, when decorating any room, that if you want to make it appear larger, use a wallpaper with a small design. To make a room look smaller, choose a paper with a large design.

Making the most of a fireplace

A fireplace always adds a great deal of charm and character to a child's bedroom. It is not only a splendid focal point, but you can turn it to practical advantage as well – even if you cannot use it as a source of heat, as its maker intended. If the fireplace still has a mantelpiece, you can use it to display your child's treasures, or hang a favourite picture or painting above it.

Few people seem to use fireplaces in bedrooms today, since most people now have more modern methods of heating, such as gas or oil-fired central heating, or electric storage heaters.

You may find that the fireplace takes up valuable wall space, or is positioned exactly where you want to put the bed. This may mean that you have no alternative but to block up the fireplace, if necessary, and remove it. The opening in the wall left by the fireplace can be used to house fitted shelves, and by adding a pair of doors you will have a small fitted cupboard. This will mean you can keep the mantelpiece, and use it as a shelf.

Decorating the doors

Doors are an important feature in every room. If you are lucky enough to have well-proportioned panelled doors, you might want to strip them down to the natural wood. Then you can wax them, or repaint them with a special finish, and pick out the moulding in a complementary or contrasting colour. Remember to pay attention to the handle. A simple painted wooden knob invariably looks much better than a modern lever handle or plastic knob.

Plain flush doors often offer more scope than classic panelled ones, especially if you are decorating a room for a toddler. Very small children are unlikely to appreciate the pleasing lines of a perfectly proportioned door, but will love one which has been painted just for them. A flush-faced door is the perfect surface on which to paint a mural *(see pp60-1)* or a *trompe l'oeil* scene *(see pp92-3)*, giving you a marvellous opportunity to incorporate the door in the decorative scheme of the whole room. An unusual alternative is to cover the door in cork tiles, turning it into a giant pinboard.

For an older child, you can create your own panelled door from one which is flush-faced. You can buy moulding and pin it on the door, or paint on a design to simulate moulding. But whether you have a plain or panelled door, remember that it will offer you tremendous scope as a designer.

Disguising a radiator

Radiators vary in size according to their age. Modern ones are trim and slim, and are best decorated in colours that merge in with the walls. Use special heat-resistant aluminium paint. If you have old-fashioned radiators, which are cumbersome and ugly, you could box them in, and cover the front with a decorative grille. This will also serve as a safety measure *(see pp24-5)*. Night storage heaters can also be painted with heat-resistant paint, to blend in with your design and colour scheme.

Use any wall space above the radiator or storage heater to the best effect. You could fit a set of shelves, or hang some posters or friezes.

DECORATING BASICS

Once you have made your basic plans, the next step is to decide which type of wall covering you are going to use. There are so many different kinds available that you should have no problem in choosing the one that best suits the wall surface and fits in with what you want to do. Paint is the least expensive and most simple finish to apply to walls and ceilings. There is a tremendously wide range of shades available, but if you cannot find the right one, many manufacturers will mix up an exact shade for you.

Before deciding on the colour scheme of your room, it is a good idea to bring home a paint manufacturer's colour chart. Study the colours you intend to use, and remember that some of the most attractive colour schemes are those that do not match exactly, but incorporate different tones of the same colour. You must also remember that walls reflect light, so if you use a pale green paint, it will appear much darker on the walls.

Wallpapers

There is an enormous range of wallpapers available, both in colour and type. Many of them are manufactured for specific purposes. For example, wood chip and pulp papers will disguise surface defects in the walls.

Wallpapers can be machine- or hand-printed in many different colours, designs and sizes, with plain, pre-pasted, or self-adhesive backings.

Lining papers

These papers are completely plain, with no colour and no surface texture. They are used to give a smooth surface to a bare wall, before either wallpaper or paint is applied.

Pulp papers

These are the cheapest form of wallpaper, and are similar to lining paper. However, pulps are coloured and then printed with a design.

Duplex papers

These are made of several layers of paper. They

Creative design
While you are choosing your design scheme, collect as many paint charts, swatches of fabric and wallpaper as possible, and study them at different times of the day. Through careful planning, you will be able to combine different textures and colours to obtain an exciting effect.

are therefore stronger than pulp papers and much easier to handle when wet.

Wood chip papers

Although similar to duplex papers, these contain wood chips to give even greater strength. They take paint very well, and provide a good background surface.

Flocked and embossed papers

Both of these papers are expensive, and look best in a traditional setting. Flocked papers are heavy-duty, with a design picked out in pile. Embossed papers are also thick, and feature a design which is punched out in relief.

Vinyl papers

These papers are tough, moisture-resistant, and can be scrubbed. They are therefore an excellent choice for children's rooms, since they are very durable.

Textured vinyl papers

These are plain vinyls which have been treated to resemble fabrics. They are easy to clean, hardwearing, and are cheaper than fabrics and easier to hang.

Flock vinyl papers

Similar in design to flocked wallpapers, these are vinyl papers which have a pile surface. Their vinyl composition means that they can be scrubbed.

Polythene papers

Although these look like paper, they are made of foamed plastic. They are available in many colours and designs, and are easy to hang.

Fabrics

Many types of fabrics have been used for covering walls, including hessians, silks, linens, chintzes, grasscloth and felt. When used effectively, they add their own richness to a room, which can be most appealing, and give an interesting and attractive surface to a wall.

Fabrics are very difficult to hang (although felts, hessians and silks can be bought with paper backings, which will make hanging easier), tend to be expensive and are not easy to clean. However, they give such an exotic finish that they

are well worth the extra effort. Because they easily become dirty, they are unsuitable for a toddler, but they will give an exotic finish to the room of an older child.

Types of paint

Initially choosing the right sort of paint to use can prove confusing. You can buy paint with an emulsion or oil base, and in gloss, silk or matt finishes. This means you can decorate the room in just one colour, but using different types of paint. For example, you can use a matt emulsion on the walls and a full gloss oil-based paint on the woodwork, both in the same shade. Some paints are now available which can be used for all surfaces.

Emulsion paints

These do not contain oil, and have been thinned with water. Therefore, any spills can be quickly washed away. Emulsion paints dry much faster than oil-based paints, so are ideal if you wish to decorate a room in a hurry.

Oil-based paints

Since these paints dry to a hard, washable finish, they are more hard-wearing, longer-lasting, and much easier to clean than emulsions. However, they take at least eight hours to dry. They are always used for wood or metal surfaces, and can be used on walls to give an exciting finish.

Paint finishes

Both types of paint are available in various degrees of sheen, from full gloss to matt. However, high-gloss emulsion paints do not give such a high sheen as oil-based paints with a similar finish. You must also remember that a more glossy oil-based paint will emphasize any existing surface defects more than a glossy emulsion paint.

Another point to consider is the paint that may already be on the wall. An oil-based paint can be used over an emulsion, but not vice versa, because the paint will not 'take' – use a matt or silk finish oil-based paint instead.

Painting techniques

There are many special, yet subtle, effects which can be applied to both furniture and walls. With practice and patience, they can be achieved by the amateur to give a professional finish.

Exciting painting techniques can be used equally well on walls as furniture. It has become increasingly fashionable to have dragged, stippled, sponged, rag-rolled or marbled walls, and these special finishes can look marvellous on furniture too. You can decorate the finished surface when the paint is dry.

Giving a coat of paint to an old or dull piece of furniture can transform it into an attractive feature which blends in with the rest of the room. Suitable pieces for decoration include chests of drawers, tables, chairs and wardrobes.

Preparing the piece of furniture

For successful results, all surfaces must be clean, dry and reasonably sound. New or unpainted wood will need to be primed, while old paintwork which is in good condition will only require a thorough wash with a household cleaner. Any paint that is in bad condition must be removed, which will take time. Rub down gloss paint with medium- or fine-grade glass-paper, and remove old varnish with steel wool and white spirit.

Before you start work, you must check the furniture for any problems, such as chips or small indentations in the wood. You can fill these in with a proprietary wood filler, and then sand them down when dry. If the furniture has woodworm, this must be treated, or it can spread to other wooden objects in the room and infect them. Treat the woodworm with a proprietary killer, following the manufacturer's instructions, and keep it away from young children and animals. You can then fill in any obvious holes with a proprietary wood filler.

Remove any handles, and keep them in a safe place, with their accompanying screws. Fix a screw or nail into the bottom of each leg of a chair or table, to raise it slightly, so that your paint brush does not pick up any dust or fluff. Larger pieces of furniture are more easily painted if they are raised on battens. Remember when working on tables and chairs to paint the undersides first.

Try to work in a secluded, dust-free place, as you will have to allow sufficient time for each coat of paint to dry. It is also a good idea to cover the floor of your working area with a dust sheet or some newspaper. Painting can be very messy, and you will inevitably have splashes.

Preparing walls

Paint applied to dirty or crumbling walls will not adhere properly. It is therefore essential to make the surface you wish to paint as clean and dry as possible. Dust all the surfaces to be painted before you begin, to remove dirt and cobwebs.

Wash down the walls and woodwork, using a mild soap or detergent, and then go over them with clean water to remove any streaks. You must fill in any cracks and holes in the walls with a proprietary filler, to give a smooth surface, then sand them down and dust them off. If you are painting over an existing wallpaper, brush it well to clean it, and make sure that it is not peeling or torn. You will be able to stick down the odd corner, but will have to completely remove paper which is in a bad condition. A glossy, decorative finish will only highlight any faults in the walls. If using an oil-based paint, whether over plaster or paper, you must apply an undercoat first, to give a good key for the paint.

Applying a flat colour to furniture

First, apply a coat of primer if working on new or unpainted wood. When it is completely dry, apply the first of the three top coats of the paint you have chosen. Remember not to put too much paint on your brush, and always draw it outwards towards an edge.

Leave the paint to dry for a minimum of 12 to 16 hours, although it is better to leave it for a whole day if possible. When the paint is completely dry, lightly rub it down with fine-grade glass paper, and dust it, before applying the next coat of paint. Although this is time-consuming, it will give a much better finish than if you apply just one layer of top coat. When the second coat is dry, repeat the rubbing-down process before applying the final coat of paint. You can paint motifs on top of this finish or leave it plain.

Preparing for a special technique

For all of the painting techniques, you need a special brush, sponge, or rags, and a coloured scumble glaze you will have prepared yourself. The wall or furniture which you want to decorate must be painted first, to give a good background on which to work. To get the best results, use a flat or mid-sheen oil-based paint. The colour you choose will depend on your design, but a good background is white or an off-white shade.

Brushes

Always buy the best brushes you can afford, as they make all the difference to the finished result. The best-quality brushes are made from hog

bristle, while the cheaper variety are made from a mixture of natural and synthetic fibres. A good-quality brush will have relatively long bristles, which taper to a thin wedge when the brush is loaded with paint.

Brushes are measured by the width of their heads, and range from 12mm (½in) to beyond 100mm (4in). You will find that a set of four will adequately serve for most jobs. Buy one of each of the following sizes: 12mm (½in), 25mm (1in), 50mm (2in) and 100mm (4in). Use the largest size to paint walls and ceilings.

After using a brush, you must clean it according to the type of paint you have been using. When using an oil-based paint, clean off the worst of the paint with white spirit, then leave the brush to soak for a few minutes in a proprietary brush cleaner fluid, as this keeps the bristles soft. Emulsion paint can be washed off in running water, before the brush is soaked in brush cleaner fluid. When you want to re-use a brush, rinse it in warm water, and then shake the brush

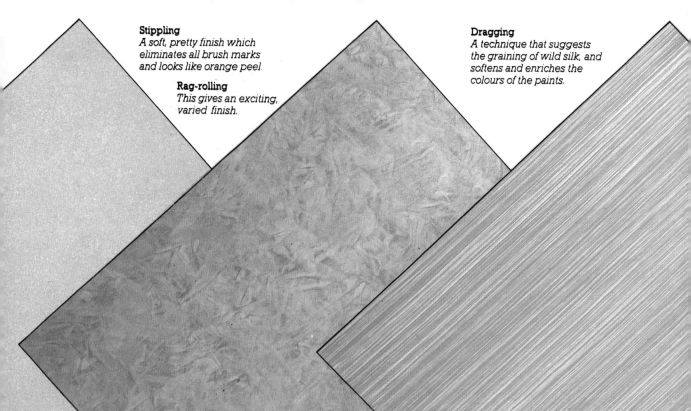

Stippling
A soft, pretty finish which eliminates all brush marks and looks like orange peel.

Rag-rolling
This gives an exciting, varied finish.

Dragging
A technique that suggests the graining of wild silk, and softens and enriches the colours of the paints.

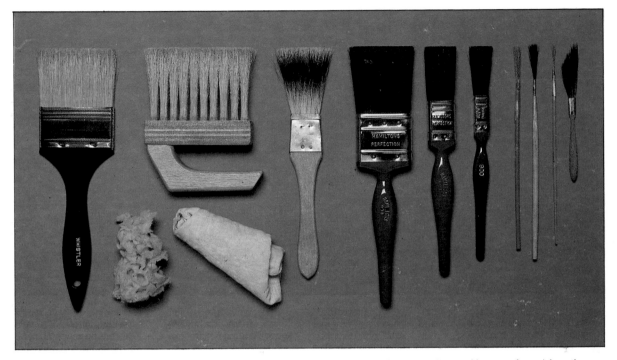

Decorating equipment
Here is the equipment for the techniques on the following two pages. From

left to right: a flogger (walnut stippler) for dragging; a natural sponge for sponging; a stippling

brush for stippling; a rag for rag-rolling; a badger brush for marbling; three decorating brushes for

glazes and varnishes; three lining brushes for marbling; a sword-liner for making straight lines.

Sponging
The easiest of all the special effects to create, sponging gives an interesting texture.

Marbling
This gives an unusual finish, and the technique can be loosely based on a real piece of marble.

thoroughly to remove most of the moisture from it.

Never leave a brush soaking in cleaner or white spirit for days, as the bristles will weaken. When you have finished painting, clean your brush, allow the bristles to dry naturally, having smoothed them down, then wrap the brush in paper and store flat in a dry place.

Using a test board
Before you begin using the glaze, practise on a piece of board painted with your background colour. This will help you to become used to the particular technique you wish to use, and also to check that the final colour combination is satisfactory. If possible, leave the board overnight, before beginning painting. You will know if you have added enough varnish by the length of time the glaze takes to dry.

Scumble glaze
Before beginning work, prepare the scumble glaze you will need for the special techniques of dragging, stippling, sponging, rag-rolling and marbling. You will find a paint kettle with a lid invaluable for mixing the various constituents, and its lid will mean your finished glaze will keep for weeks without going off.

To two parts of scumble glaze, which you can buy in specialist decorating stores, add one part of white eggshell paint and stir well with a wooden stick until the glaze has the consistency of cream. It can then be tinted to the colour of your choice. This is best done by adding a liquid colour, known as a stainer (tinting colour), which is available in specialist paint stores. It is very concentrated, so add a very little at a time, and stir well. Remember you can make the colour stronger, but you cannot weaken it, unless you dilute the glaze with more scumble glaze and white eggshell.

If you wish, add about a tablespoon of varnish to 0.5 litre (1 pint) of scumble glaze, which will act as both a drying agent and a hardener. Always err on the side of caution, since too much varnish will take a very long time to dry.

Dragging
Flogger brush (walnut stippler)
100-mm (4-in) wide paint brush
Prepared scumble glaze
Clear matt varnish

You will need a special brush, known as a flogger (walnut stippler). It is made from long, top-quality bristles with special split ends. You can use a wide, standard bristle brush, but the flogger gives a better finish. Paint on your coloured glaze with the wide paint brush, keeping your strokes running in one direction. This is known as 'laying off in one direction'.

Draw the flogger down the wet paint in a straight line. When dragging the next section, overlap the lines of brush strokes slightly. Wipe your brush on some old rags as the paint builds up. Allow plenty of time for the glaze to dry, then varnish with the cleaned wide brush. Be careful which varnish you use, as some will make the colour turn yellow with age.

Rag-rolling
Clean folded rags
Prepared scumble glaze
100-mm (4-in) wide paint brush
Metal dustbin with lid
Clear matt varnish

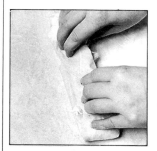

Before you begin, collect sufficient clean, dry rags of the same material. Old sheets or pillow cases are best, but avoid any rag with a seam. Practise on a painted test board, experimenting rolling rags in different ways. When you have chosen a method, make sure that you roll all the rags in the same way, or you will get a variety of finishes. Lay off the glaze in one direction, using a wide paint brush.

Quickly press a folded rag over the wet glaze, using a rolling movement (see top), or dab at the glaze with a rolled-up rag (see above). Use a fresh rag when the old one becomes impregnated with glaze. When you discard them, place your highly flammable rags in a metal dustbin with a lid. Apply a clear matt varnish when the glaze is dry.

Stippling

Stippling brush
100-mm (4-in) wide paint
brush
Prepared scumble glaze
Clear matt varnish

*You will need a special
stippling brush, which
resembles a shaving brush,
or you can make do with a
decorator's dusting brush.
Stippling brushes are
available in a variety of sizes,
according to the size of the
area you wish to decorate.
Lay off the glaze in one
direction using the wide
paint brush. Then, holding
the stippling brush at right
angles to the surface, dab at
the wet glaze in short, sharp
movements, until you are
happy with the result. An
alternative method is to
stipple the glaze directly on
to the base colour. Allow the
glaze to dry and then apply a
clear matt varnish.*

Sponging

Clean sponge
Prepared scumble glaze
100-mm (4-in) wide paint
brush
Clear matt varnish

*Buy a natural sponge, the
size of which will depend on
the surface area you wish to
cover. Remember that a
sponge has two distinct
sides, one more open than
the other, which will provide
different effects. Experiment
with them on your painted
board before beginning
sponging. Using a paint
brush, load the sponge with
glaze, then dab it on to a
piece of paper to remove
any surplus paint. Next, dab
the glaze on to the painted
surface in a circular motion,
working up the colour so
that it blends together
evenly. If you want to
introduce a third colour,
work it in with a separate
sponge. When the glaze is
completely dry, apply a
clear, matt varnish, using the
wide paint brush. Clean the
sponge in white spirit, then
rinse in washing-up liquid
and warm water.*

Marbling

Prepared scumble glaze
Clean, dry rags
Crumpled soft paper
Stippling brush
Badger brush
Lining brushes
Artists' oil colour
Turpentine
Matt and gloss varnish
French chalk
Clean, soft cloth

*Before you start, study some
genuine pieces of marble to
see how the veining runs, so
that you will be able to get
the right effect. As always,
practise marbling first on
your sample board,
checking that the colours
you have chosen blend
together correctly. Paint the
surface to be marbled with
scumble glaze, using the
wide paint brush. Then mix
up the colours for the veins
by tinting the glaze with oil
paints, then thinning this
with turpentine. Dab on
blobs of paint at random
then, using the stipple brush,
blend them together.*

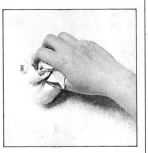

*Then work on the surface
with a piece of crumpled soft
paper, creating cracks and
ridges in the glaze.*

*Take a badger brush and
soften the glaze by brushing
it over the surface in a light
flicking motion.*

*Then begin to paint on the
veins, with the glaze mixed
with oil paints, and using a
lining brush with very long
bristles. Hold the brush
gently at an angle of about
45° to the surface, and twist
it. As the bristles move, they
will flop over to form
random lines. Soften these
with the badger brush. Add a
little more colour if
necessary.*

*Soften the lines again using a
clean piece of crumpled
paper. Continue painting on
veins to build up the
marbling. and then soften
them with the badger brush
and crumped paper until
you are happy with the
effect.*

*Finally, add some veins in a
dark colour to give depth to
the marbling. Allow to dry,
then paint on white veins,
and soften them with the
brush and paper. Once the
paint is dry, varnish, using
two parts of matt varnish to
one part of gloss varnish.
When this is almost dry,
sprinkle it with French chalk.
Polish this off with a clean,
soft cloth.*

CREATIVE COLOUR

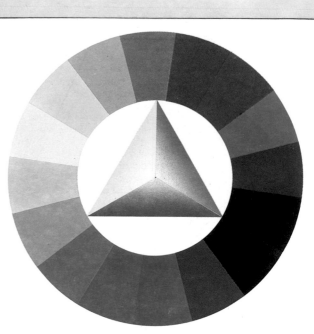

A colour wheel is like a rainbow, as it is made up of primary and secondary colours. On the wheel, a secondary colour lies between two primary colours which, when combined, produce it.

Colour is a life-giver. Without it, our lives would be dull and flat, and a strong love of colour is within us all. As we become older, however, conservatism takes over, we are more inhibited, and less bold, in our use of colour. Children have the completely opposite approach. They love bright, vivid colours. So when you decorate a child's room, seize the opportunity to use plenty of them.

Choosing the colour scheme will probably be the most important design decision you make, because it will provide the room with its most memorable feature. Be brave! Through your use of colour you should aim to express your personality, and that of your child, if he or she has been born yet.

If you intend to decorate more than one child's room in your house, choose the colour schemes one at a time. However, try to give the whole design some cohesion, perhaps by linking each room with a particular colour, or expressing one theme in different ways in every room.

Before you begin to plan your colour scheme, it will help you if you understand the relationship of the primary – red, blue and yellow – and secondary colours, by looking at a colour wheel. Within the colour spectrum, some colours harmonize, others contrast, and they can combine to produce further shades. Using two contrasting colours in a room can give drama to a design, and one main colour with a secondary shade will produce a softer, more subtle effect.

Contrasting and harmonizing colours

When incorporating two contrasting colours in your decorative scheme, do not use them in equal amounts. Choose a main colour for the dominant features in the room, such as the walls, flooring and curtains. Then use the contrasting colour for the binding on the curtains, for piping, cushions and lampshades, and decorating furniture, to set off the main colour. If two contrasting colours are used in equal amounts, they tend to fight, and can be tiring to the eyes.

Creating a mood with colour

Different colours will create different moods in a room, making it peaceful and gentle, or vibrant and lively. The light in the room and the colours you use are interrelated. A room with a poor source of light may become depressing if it is decorated in a dark tone, but will be cheerful if you use a bright colour.

Warm and cold colours

Warm colours draw in walls, ceilings and floors, so will diminish the spacious feeling which a room might otherwise have. Similarly, cool colours make a room appear larger than it really is.

When you are choosing the colour for your decorative scheme, you must consider which time of the day the room is used most. If it is full of sunlight during the day, but will be used principally in the evening, do not decorate it in the cool colour you would normally choose for a sunny room. The artificial lighting in the evenings will make the room feel too cold. Remember that electric light enhances warm colours, and makes cool colours seem even colder.

Reds
Rich and warm. Paler shades of reds and pinks are warm but softer. They enhance rooms which have a poor source of natural light.

Blues
Cool and restful. These shades are ideal for sunny rooms.

Yellows
Bright and light, and good in the dark areas of a room.

Greens
Cool and calming. A green tinged with blue becomes colder, and is suitable for sunny rooms. A green tinged with yellow is warmer, and can be used in dark rooms.

Oranges and browns
Warm and cosy, but they need a good contrasting colour to enliven them. These are suitable colours for dark rooms.

Purples and greys
Warm but formal. Paler shades, in mauve, can be soft and subtle. They are effective in bright rooms.

CHILD SAFETY

By now, you will have begun to plan how to decorate your child's room, and you may have a clear picture of what it will look like. However, there is one final, important consideration – safety. Design features which are suitable for an older child may be very unsafe for a four-year old.

Power points

Small children are extremely inquisitive, and love playing with strange objects. An electrical power point, therefore, can be just one more toy to play with. Although you will tell your child not to touch a point, you may be uneasy about leaving him or her alone with a potentially dangerous object. One answer is to make the power points child-proof, so that even if your warnings go unheeded, your child will still not come to any harm.

An ideal solution is to install electric sockets at a height of at least 1.3m (4 ft) above the floor. This will put them out of reach of your toddler, who will not be able to play with them.

If this is impractical, a sensible alternative is to install a shuttered electric socket which only opens when a plug is pushed into it, and has an on-off switch. Some children have the terrifying habit of trying to push metal objects which they have found, such as knitting needles, into power points.

Safe heating

It is very important to consider the form of heating you will use in your child's room. Some methods of heating, which are used for adults with barely a second thought, are quite unsuitable for small children.

Roaring log or coal fires add great character to a room, and will make it very warm and welcoming. However, such a fire in a toddler's room can be a real danger, unless it is surrounded by a strong fire guard, and an adult keeps a constant close watch on the child. Many houses are heated with gas or oil-fired central heating, or electric storage heaters. Radiators can become very hot to the touch, and might burn a small child. It is therefore best to box in radiators, building a simple wooden surround, and covering the front in a pretty metal or wooden grille. If you cover the interior of the box with special foil, which can be bought for the purpose, this will reflect the heat back into the room.

Never put an electric fire with exposed elements into a child's room, and ensure that other heating appliances are in proper working order and are not left unattended for long periods. Remember, too, to keep electrical flexes tidy. If they are allowed to trail over the floor, they can get caught up in a child's legs, with disastrous consequences.

Securing windows

Make sure that your windows are child-proof. Unless you are completely gutting a room, it is unlikely that you will want to replace your windows, so you must make the existing ones as safe as possible.

Put safety catches on the window frames, so they can be locked shut, or opened a little way but no further. As an alternative, you could fit vertical wood or metal bars across the windows, which will also serve as a deterrent to potential burglars.

Stabilizing furniture and rugs

Ensure that all the furniture in the room is stable, and not easily knocked over. Another danger is furniture that is top-heavy, and could easily fall on to your child. When installing a set of shelves, fix them securely to the wall, to stop them falling forward if too much weight is applied to the top of them.

When your child is young, you might prefer to cover bare floorboards, or cork tiles, with a few rugs, rather than invest in an expensive fitted carpet which may be spoiled. If so, make sure the rugs do not slip, by fitting non-slip strips to the undersides.

Sensible bedding

A baby will sleep in a cot or bassinet when very small. It is very important to give your child a wipeable safety mattress, without a pillow. This is because if the mattress is soft, your baby's head will dent it. Then, if your baby is sick while sleeping, he or she may suffocate in the pool of vomit which will collect in the dent. Equally, your child could suffocate while sleeping with a pillow.

If you want to buy, or renovate, a cot, you must ensure that it is safe for your child. A new cot should bear a label saying it has passed standard safety tests. However, if you are using an old cot, check that the wood is sound and smooth. If it is infested with woodworm, you must treat this with a proprietary woodworm killer. A metal cot should be made of aluminium or stainless steel and be resistant to corrosion. Check the struts to ensure that they are a safe distance apart, and not so close together that your baby's fingers can get caught between them, and not so far apart that your child's head could slide between them.

By making and fitting a simple, washable, buffer to the inside of the cot, you can ensure that your child does not come to harm on the bars. Make it fit along the head and foot of the cot, and secure it to the bars with ribbons. A buffer will also act as a good draught-excluder.

Very small children sleep in cots, but they usually graduate to beds by the age of two. When buying your child's first bed, choose one with a firm mattress. Remember that a toddler's spine is still growing, and must be firmly supported while the child is asleep.

You may decide to buy bunk beds, as these provide more play area in a bedroom that is shared by two children. However, they are not suitable for children under the age of five. The great attraction of bunk beds for children is the excitement of sleeping on the top bed, and toddlers can easily fall out and on to the floor.

Keeping the lighting simple

Small children are fascinated by trailing electrical flexes, and may become entangled in them while playing. This can cause accidents which vary from the annoying to the serious. You should therefore reduce this risk by not giving your very young child a bedside light. Instead, a central ceiling light is the best method of lighting the room of any child up to the age of five.

If your child is frightened of the dark, buy an attractive child-proof nightlight. You can put it in the bedroom before your child goes to sleep.

Safe decorations

Never underestimate a toddler's ability to try to eat everything in sight! Objects which you would never even consider tasting, will appear extremely appetizing to your child.

Therefore, you must consider the type of paint you wish to use to decorate your child's room. Toddlers who are teething enjoy chewing pieces of furniture, and even doors, so make sure that you use non-toxic, lead-free paints!

Remember, too, not to decorate a small child's room with little toys or ornaments which could be easily swallowed. Beware also of long pieces of material or string, such as those on a mobile, which could become wrapped around a child's neck.

Safeguarding against animals

If you own a cat, and have a baby, you must ensure against accidents. For example, if you leave your baby sleeping, and the door open, your cat could jump into the cot, and suffocate your child by sitting on his or her face. You can prevent this by always shutting the cat out of the nursery, and buying or making a net cover that fits over the top of the pram, but allows the baby to breathe normally.

Protecting a toddler

Once your child learns how to walk, you must make absolutely sure that the house is as safe as possible. One danger is that of your child falling down the stairs. You can prevent this by fitting sturdy low gates at the top and bottom of the stairs, locking them when necessary.

YOUR NURSERY

Golden slumbers kiss your eyes,
Smiles awake you when you rise.
Sleep, pretty wantons, do not cry,
And I will sing a lullaby:
Rock them, rock them, lullaby.

Care is heavy, therefore sleep you;
You are care, and care must keep you.
Sleep, pretty wantons, do not cry,
And I will sing a lullaby:
Rock them, rock them, lullaby.

A Cradle Song

Thomas Dekker
1572?-1632

Transform a simple nursery into something special with a mural.

CONTENTS

WHAT EVERY BABY NEEDS

One of the joys of expecting a baby is planning the nursery. Babies thrive in a clean, hygienic atmosphere, but need stimuli right from the start. Make a list of all the pieces of furniture you will need, which will help you to design the room so it can be as functional as possible, while combining an atmosphere of warmth and welcome for your baby. In the early stages of your child's life, he or she will only need a few essential pieces of furniture *(see pp32-3)*, and some storage space, for clothes and toys.

Always allow yourself plenty of time. Do not leave all the decoration until the last couple of months, because as your pregnancy progresses, you will become larger and may tire easily. Also, you will begin to worry that the nursery will not be ready in time, and this will detract from your pleasure in its planning. And remember that babies can arrive early!

Make it friendly

As you will probably not know whether your baby will be a boy or a girl, you must make the room suitable for a child of either sex.

If you have decided to paint the walls of the nursery, I believe that the only colour you should avoid is pink, unless you know your baby is going to be a girl. While you can easily put a girl into a blue room, I feel that pink is such a feminine colour that it is unfair to ask a boy to live with it!

If you choose a wallpaper for your baby's room, pick one with a motif that is not overpowering. Make sure that, if the paper portrays characters, they look friendly, and are figures that your child will grow to love. You will then be able to invent bedtime stories around them when your child is older. Pick out some of the characters and use them elsewhere in the room, such as painting them on a lampshade *(see pp84-5)*, or making a simple mobile and hanging them above the cot or nappy-changing area as decorations.

Babies soon develop a sense of identity with their nurseries, and find them a relaxing influence. In order to stimulate and develop your child's mind, decorate the room with plenty of pictures, toys and mobiles, that your baby will soon begin to recognize and enjoy. The room will become a treasure trove of early memories, so it should be bright, airy, cosy and comforting: a room which creates an atmosphere of peace and well-being.

Introducing organization

There is nothing worse than looking about for a missing safety pin or tub of cream while your baby is crying, the telephone is ringing, the kettle is boiling and there is someone at the door. To save your time and your nerves, organize the nursery so that you have everything you need to hand. For example, you can fit a set of shelves near the area in which you change nappies, and fill them with the equipment you will need. They will then be within easy reach. Paint the shelves to blend in with the rest of the room.

An alternative is to paint and decorate an old trolley. It will provide useful storage space for all the baby care equipment you need, with the added advantage that you will be able to wheel it from the nursery to the bathroom as you wish.

Choosing the curtains

When you come to choose the curtain material, bear in mind that babies are very sensitive to light. Some fabrics are so fine that, unless the curtains are properly lined, strong daylight can filter through them and wake up your baby when he or she should be sleeping.

A young child also has morning and afternoon naps, and you will want to be able to darken the room equally well in summer and winter. The best way of doing this is to inter-line, as well as line, the curtains. You can also make your own blinds, following the instructions on the facing page. Closely-woven fabrics, such as cotton, linen or canvas, are the best fabrics to use, as they are firm and roll easily. PVC sheeting and vinyl are also suitable.

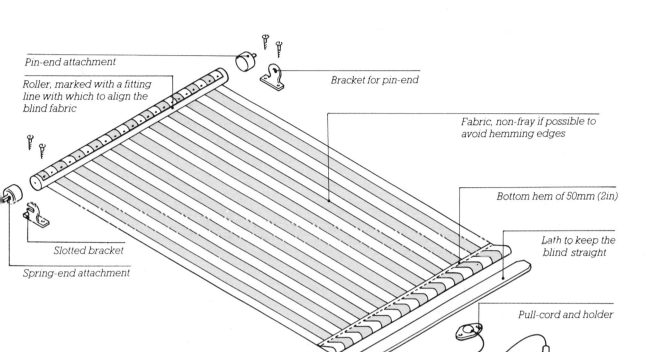

Pin-end attachment

Roller, marked with a fitting line with which to align the blind fabric

Bracket for pin-end

Fabric, non-fray if possible to avoid hemming edges

Bottom hem of 50mm (2in)

Lath to keep the blind straight

Slotted bracket

Spring-end attachment

Pull-cord and holder

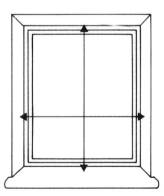

Measuring a window for a blind

If the blind is to hang inside the window recess, measure the width and length of the window (above). The finished blind should just overlap the sides and should be 160mm (6⅜in) longer than the length of the window.

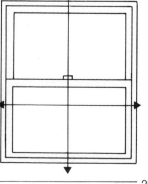

If the blind is to hang outside the window recess (below) measure the length and width of the recess. The blind should overlap the recess by about 75mm (3in) on each side, and should be 160mm (6⅜in) longer than it. The roller should be positioned 75mm (3in) above the recess.

In both of the above situations, the roller for the blind, excluding pins, should be as wide as the blind itself.

Making the blind

Roller kits contain all you need to make a blind, except the fabric. Canvas and linen are the most suitable materials. You will also need a hammer, tacks, screws, contact glue, a sewing machine and scissors.

Cut your fabric to size. Unless you use non-fray material, sew a 25-mm (1-in) hem on both long sides. Sew a hem of 50mm (2in) on the bottom of the blind. Fit the lath inside and slip stitch the open ends closed. Thread the pull-cord through its holder and screw the holder to the centre of the back of the lath.

Lay the fabric right side up. Place the roller at the top edge. Align the top edge of the fabric with the fitting line on the roller. Fix the fabric to the roller with tacks and glue.

Fitting the brackets

Attach the brackets to the end of the roller, and hold the roller in position, just above the window if there is no recess, 75mm (3in) above it if there is one. Mark the position of the bracket at the pin-end of the roller with a pencil. Take the roller down, and screw the bracket in place.

Insert the pin-end into the fitted bracket, and hold the roller in position again. Fit the spring-end into the slotted bracket. Check that the roller is straight with a set square. Mark the position of the second bracket. Remove the roller and screw the bracket in place.

Check that the blind covers the window and that the blind will lock in position, and roll up when pulled gently. If it does not, rewind the fabric on the roller to adjust the tension.

PETER RABBIT'S NURSERY

In a small bedroom, space is usually at a premium, but, with a little imagination, you can turn this apparent defect into an advantage. Here, I faced a fairly dark junk room, with only one small window, which was to be transformed into a stylish nursery. My first aim was to get as much light into the decorative scheme as possible; I also wanted to create a 'unisex' look, suitable for a boy or a girl.

The next step was to assess what part, if any, the room's existing features can play in the scheme. A fireplace can be made a striking talking-point; an unsightly door can be camouflaged, as here, by integrating it with the wall decoration. Having blocked off the fireplace to avoid draughts, I decided that I could use *trompe l'oeil (see pp92-3)* to great effect to create a 'false' fire shovel and the little miniatures above the mantelpiece.

Remember that carrying over decorative ideas on to furniture and fabrics can be extremely effective. Here, for instance, I used simple motifs to transform the rocking chair.

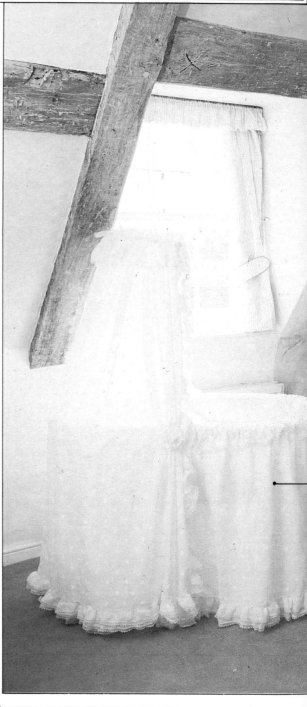

Painting a chair
Even the most ordinary rocking chair can be transformed into something completely original. I stencilled the flowers on to the chair back, then added border lines.

Making a mural
I drew these figures straight on to the wall and then painted them. If you think this is beyond your scope, you could stencil the figures on to the wall, or trace on the outlines, and then fill them in with paint.

Painting on pictures
If you can't find a suitable picture to hang on a wall, why not paint one yourself – but as a trompe l'oeil. All three pictures are 'fakes', but I painted the frames to create the illusion of light and shade, based on the angles at which natural light falls from the window.

Working round the fireplace
This fireplace has been blocked up to make it draught-proof, so I decided to use it in other ways to make it attractive. The painted fire shovel brings the plain white surround to life, I put some small ornaments on the mantelpiece, and camouflaged the empty grate by ranging lots of toys around it.

Choosing a bassinet
By using a bassinet instead of a cot for the first few months of your baby's life, you can transform a nursery into something individual and different. Here, the bassinet is a natural focal point. I draped it with a floaty fabric to accentuate the fairy tale quality of the room.

NURSERY FURNITURE

A baby needs very little furniture: a cot or bassinet, a chest of drawers in which to keep your child's clothes, a wardrobe, something on which to place a nappy changer *(see p36)*, and a nursing chair in which you can sit while feeding your baby will be your basic requirements. In addition, you will need some shelves. The most important point to remember when choosing any nursery furniture is that everything you use must be sturdy, well-made, and safe for your child, with no sharp points or protruding nails *(see pp32-3)*.

Once you have decided on the basic pieces of furniture you need for your nursery, you may find that you already own some which are ideal, but need a face-lift. Throughout this book I have shown you how to transform even the simplest piece of furniture into something that is exciting and original, using special painting techniques, stencils and transfers *(see pp14-21, 40-1, 44-5, 100-1, 112-3)*.

It is more than likely that friends and relations will offer you old items of furniture that they no longer need, which you can renovate yourself. If you do have to buy furniture, make sure that it is of the best quality you can afford.

What do you need?

At this stage in your child's life, a lot of the furniture in the baby's room is more for your use than that of your baby. Once your child becomes a toddler, you will be able to remove some of the objects in the room, such as the nappy changer. A nursing chair is an important piece of furniture in a nursery. You will spend a great deal of time feeding your baby, and you should be as comfortable as possible while you do so. Most people find a fairly low, armless, upholstered chair the most practical choice. It will show less dirt if you cover it in a patterned fabric, which blends with the rest of the room – plain material shows up the slightest mark. Do make sure that

the fabric you choose can be scrubbed, so that you can clean it when accidents happen.

If you are not breast-feeding, you will find it saves time to have a table or trolley, which you can paint to look attractive, within easy reach of the nursing chair, filled with all the equipment you will need. The time when you feed your child should be a peaceful one for both of you, and you will feel frustrated if you have to keep stopping to cross the room to fetch something you need.

Even at this age, your baby will need some storage space, for both clothes and toys. You will be able to keep some clothes in the chest of drawers, and hang up others in the wardrobe. If this has fitted shelves they may be all the storage you need for your baby's toys. Later, you can buy or make a toy chest *(see pp52-3)*.

Suitable bedding for your baby

Some mothers prefer not to put their newborn babies straight into a cot, and give them a bassinet instead. However, whichever bedding you use must be safe *(see pp24-5)*.

All babies sleep in cots sooner or later, so try to make yours as individual as your baby. If you want to buy, or renovate, a cot, after checking that it is suitable, you can paint and then decorate it as you wish. You could decorate it with the motif you are using in the room, or paint on your child's name. Choose sheets and blankets in a colour that blends in with the room.

A bassinet is a basket on a stand, draped in a soft fabric which falls to the floor in folds, and is smaller and cosier than a cot. As a result, it can only be used for the first few months of your baby's life, until he or she grows out of it, so it is something of a luxury. Nevertheless, a bassinet can transform an ordinary nursery into something different and unusual.

Instead of keeping your baby's pyjamas or sleepsuit in a drawer, you can make a special pyjama holder. A stuffed toy, which has a pocket inside it in which to keep pyjamas, can be hung on the door of your baby's room. The instructions for this are given on the facing page.

Cutting out the pattern

Enlarge your chosen animal shape to a suitable size. The body must be large enough for a pocket of about 400mm (10in) square to hold the pyjamas. Trace the main outline of the animal's body on to gridded pattern paper.

Move the tracing to a new part of the pattern paper, and transfer the outlines of all the other features. Draw the pocket shape on about 10mm (²/₈in) smaller all round than the pattern piece for the animal's body. Cut out all pattern pieces.

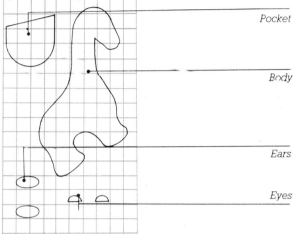

Pocket

Body

Ears

Eyes

Making the pyjama holder

Fold the fabric in half, right sides together. Pin the pattern pieces to the folded fabric, and cut them out, so that you have two pieces of fabric for each pattern piece.

Pin the two main body pieces right sides together. Machine a 16-mm (⁵/₈-in) seam around the edge, leaving a suitable gap in which to fit the pocket. For example, if your pocket is 400mm (10in) wide, leave a gap of 400mm (10in) in the seam. To make the mane sew a 12-mm (¹/₂-in) hem on 75-mm (2-in) wide strip of material. Gather it and sew it into the seam on the neck.

Pin the pocket pieces, right sides together. Machine a 16mm (⁵/₈in) seam on three sides, and

tack a hem of 16mm (⁵/₈in) hem around the fourth.

Turn the animal right sides out, and fill the limbs, with fireproof toy stuffing, available from haberdashery shops. Fit the pocket inside the body. Pin, tack and machine a zip in the opening of the pocket.

The finishing touches

Sew on the features. Do not use buttons or anything else a small child may pull off and swallow. Add any hair or whiskers by sewing wool through the fabric and knotting the two loose ends.

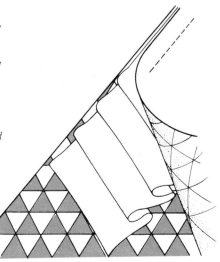

THE CLASSIC TOUCH

In bigger rooms, there is generally more light to play with, and the proportions should normally not present much of a problem. What may be difficult is creating a personality for the room that suits you – and, of course, your child. Like older children, babies respond to atmosphere and big rooms can lack soul.

.Rather than devising a major decorative scheme, I decided here that I could create just as much individuality by concentrating on points of detail. Built-in standard fittings can be given that personal touch by hand-painting them with simple decorative motifs. I brightened up the alcove with a *trompe l'oeil (see pp92-3)*.

You will see that the painted motifs on the chest of drawers are taken from the wallpaper I chose for the room. I did this simply by tracing off the design before hanging the paper. Once you have the trace, you can use it for all sorts of purposes – you could use it as a pattern for decorative embroidery, for example.

Brightening up shelves
I changed the concept of a simple set of shelves by painting a trompe l'oeil behind them and fitting them with glass shelves.

Using decorations

A mobile hung over the nappy-changing area will keep your baby happy – and will make changing a soiled nappy that much easier!

Fitting a basin

If you have the space, you will find a basin invaluable in a nursery. As I did here, incorporate it into the design of the room, building fitted cupboards below, for spare towels and washing equipment, or just for use as an extra storage space.

Individualizing furniture

This chest of drawers is very simple in design, but imaginative decoration has made it look exciting and different, while retaining the classic feel of the room.

Q for queen

Incorporate the letters of the alphabet in your design, to help your child learn to read.

YOUR NURSERY

A NAPPY CHANGER

Every mother with a young baby knows that nappies are an inevitable part of life. However, with a nappy changer you can relieve much of the burden of this chore. The changer is made of plywood, and you can adjust its size so that it fits on top of the table or chest of drawers in your own nursery.

Taking the measurements

Measure the width and length of your chosen surface, measuring from the outermost edges. To these width and length measurements, add 40mm (1⅗in) to both to give you the length and width of the bottom *(1)* of the changer; the extra size allows the changer to fit easily in place. The length of the front and back *(2 and 3)* of the changer should be the same as the length of the bottom *(1)* plus an extra 24mm (1in) for making the joints. The length of the two sides *(4)* should be the same as the width of the bottom, plus 12mm (½in), to allow for the joints. When complete, the changer normally has a lower rim of 60mm (2⅖in), to hold it securely in place. Make sure this is adequate *(see diagram)*. If not, adjust the width of the front, back and sides.

Making the changer

Mark out all the pieces on the plywood with a pencil and a ruler. Saw them out. Mark and saw out the recesses in the front, back and sides *(2,3 and 4)*.

Fitting the changer together

With a ruler, draw a line along the front, back and sides of the changer, 125mm (5in) down from the top edge. Fix the support battens *(5 and 6)* along the lines with wood glue and panel pins. Saw a groove 12mm (½in) wide and 6mm (¼in) deep at each end of the front and back *(2 and 3)* for the joints.

Countersink holes for the screws, using a drill and countersink bit, in the grooved joints. Fit the sides *(4)* into the joints and screw the corners of the changer together. Check that the corners are square with a set square. Fit the bottom *(1)* over the support battens so that it lies snugly in place. Secure the bottom to the support battens with wood glue and panel pins.

Fill in the countersink holes with proprietary wood filler, and allow it to dry. Then sand the surface until it is smooth. Paint the changer with primer, allow this to dry, and then paint it with gloss paint.

Furnishing a nursery
Furniture for a nursery must be practical as well as attractive. A nappy changer is an indispensable asset for any parent.

MATERIALS AND EQUIPMENT

Pieces

1 Bottom	1	750 x 500 x 12mm	(30 x 20 x ½in)
2 Front	1	774 x 197 x 12mm	(31 x 8 x ½in)
3 Back	1	774 x 197 x 12mm	(31 x 8 x ½in)
4 Sides	2	512 x 197 x 12mm	(20½ x 8 x ½in)
5 Battens	2	750 x 15 x 20mm	(30 x ⅗ X ⅘in)
6 Battens	2	500 x 15 x 20mm	(20 x ⅗ x ⅘in)

NB These measurements give you a changer 774 x 524mm (31 x 21in)

Equipment

Saw, hammer, drill, countersink bit, screwdriver, panel pins, screws, wood glue, sandpaper, proprietary filler, pencil for markings, ruler, set square, paintbrushes, primer, gloss paint

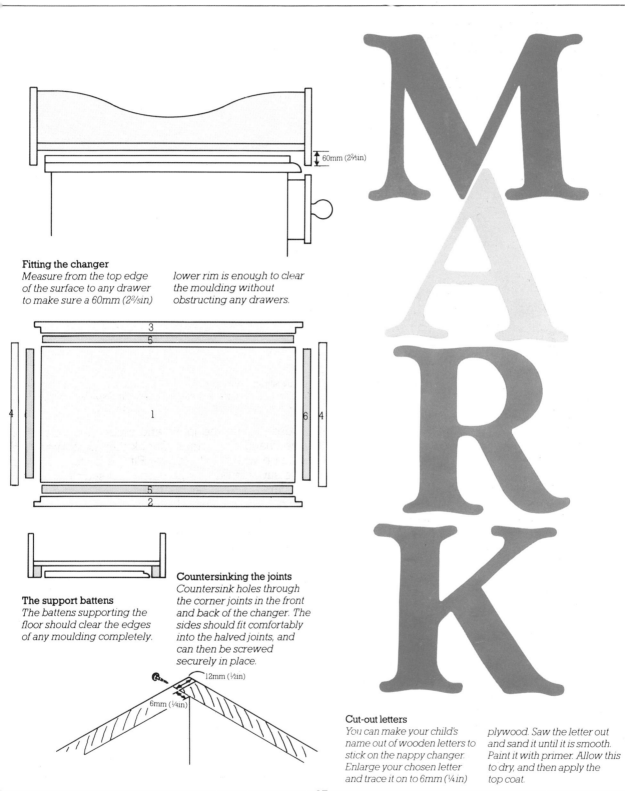

Fitting the changer
Measure from the top edge of the surface to any drawer to make sure a 60mm (2⅜in) lower rim is enough to clear the moulding without obstructing any drawers.

60mm (2⅜in)

The support battens
The battens supporting the floor should clear the edges of any moulding completely.

Countersinking the joints
Countersink holes through the corner joints in the front and back of the changer. The sides should fit comfortably into the halved joints, and can then be screwed securely in place.

12mm (½in)

6mm (¼in)

Cut-out letters
You can make your child's name out of wooden letters to stick on the nappy changer. Enlarge your chosen letter and trace it on to 6mm (¼in) plywood. Saw the letter out and sand it until it is smooth. Paint it with primer. Allow this to dry, and then apply the top coat.

NURSERY TO PLAYROOM

As your baby grows older – and becomes more active – the nursery of the days immediately after the birth has to double up as a playroom. Because of the expense this involves, I prefer to keep such transformations simple. The cot is still the dominant feature, though it is a good idea to push it back against a side wall to allow room for your baby to play. If you do this, it is important that you choose an inside-facing wall, rather than an outside-facing one, to minimize heat loss to keep the baby warm. On the cot, I added a buffer. This serves two purposes, protecting the baby against draughts and the risk of a bumped head.

When it came to the walls and ceilings, I again kept things simple, but added a touch of contrast to maintain interest. To provide that feeling of security and safety that is so important for every growing baby, I choose soft, reassuring colours for the walls. The contrast came from the pattern of colour in the ceiling above the pelmet.

The choice of fabric, too, plays an important part in the overall effect. It should be warm and comforting to give your baby an added sense of security.

A simple wardrobe
Even a baby needs a wardrobe. In this room, I painted the wardrobe white, and then added the same motifs as those on the chest of drawers – rabbits, and tiny pink hearts painted in the centre of each wooden knob.

Personalized picture
There is no doubt who this room belongs to – the letters of Charlotte's name have been turned into a picture!

Holding your child's interest
As children become older, they will need an increasing amount of visual stimulation. Hang a brightly-coloured mobile above the cot for your child to play with and watch.

Careful curtaining
The curtains that I chose for this room are pale in colour, so I had to ensure that they would not let in too much light during the day and keep the baby awake. This was done by lining the curtains and the heavy pelmet as well.

Adding colour
My aim was to keep the design of this room simple, without allowing it to become boring. The colour highlights are provided by the toys and mobiles, and the motifs on the front of the chest of drawers.

Planning ahead
Plan for the years ahead when you decorate a nursery. Although your child may be too young to use a piece of furniture when you buy it, he or she will soon grow into it. Here, I added a child's wicker chair, which is being used by a rag doll until the baby girl is old enough to sit in it herself.

FURNITURE PAINTING

Furniture decorated with original painted designs makes a delightful alternative to the more conventional variety. Transforming any piece of furniture is surprisingly easy, using the techniques of tracing and painting.

Preparing the surface

Painted wood should be sanded down, then repainted, or at least washed thoroughly.

Unpainted wood should be washed thoroughly and varnished if you wish. The colours and textures of paint on varnished wood appear brighter, and the outlines bolder than on unvarnished wood.

Metal. Any rust should be removed, and the metal repainted.

Formica, melamine and other plastics should be washed thoroughly.

Cloth is unsuitable for these decorative techniques.

Choosing a design

This can be taken from almost any source (see p128): books, comics, wallpaper, fabric, or a favourite picture are just a few possibilities. When you have traced the design you want, you can have it reduced or enlarged to a suitable size (see pp60-1), or to a variety of sizes, at a photocopying shop. Alternatively, you can reduce or enlarge it yourself by the grid method (see pp60-1). You will need a wide collection of designs in various sizes if you intend to paint several pieces of furniture with the same motifs.

Make sure that your design is neither too small nor too large for the proportions of the piece of furniture. Bear in mind that a curved surface will also affect the appearance and perspective of the design. The effect of a pattern with predominant horizontal lines, such as a ship, or a figure with outstretched arms, on table or chair legs will be destroyed.

Before decorating, draw up a complete plan of how you would like the finished product to look. Lightly trace the complete design on the piece of furniture to make sure that your idea works in practice.

Paint and brushes

Enamel model paint, available from most model or toy shops and hardware stores, is ideal. Equally effective on gloss or emulsion paint, it is tough and hard-wearing and does not need varnishing. It is also available in a wide range of colours.

Ideally, the paint should not drip when you dip a brush into it. Leaving the paints open for a few hours allows them to thicken. Tracing paper is perfect as a palate for mixing small amounts of paint, being easy to handle and disposable. Use glass jam jars for mixing larger quantities of paint. Do not use plastic containers, as some paints may melt them.

You will need art brushes of various sizes. When you finish work, always clean them immediately with turpentine or white spirit and then wash them with washing-up liquid and water. Gently smooth the bristles back to a point and store them upright.

Where and how to work

Find somewhere quiet, where no one will touch or bump into the article you are decorating. The room should be well ventilated and clean, as dust can mar the smooth surface of the paintwork.

Hold small pieces of furniture on your lap, where you can manoeuvre them easily. Try to keep the surface horizontal – painting on vertical surfaces increases the danger of the paint running, and your hand will quickly become tired. If you can steady your hand while you are working your painting will be more accurate. Remove any handles or knobs, and take out any drawers, in order to work on them individually.

Tracing the design

Find the design you wish to use, and trace all the outlines carefully on to a piece of tracing paper, using either a sharp pencil, or a very fine felt tip pen.

Turn the tracing paper over, and, using a soft pencil, scribble over all the outlines, making sure every part of the outline is well covered. Do not scribble across the whole piece of paper, as this both wastes time and increases the chances of the paintwork on the furniture becoming dirty when you transfer the tracing.

If you are tracing a design on to a surface that is painted in a dark colour, you may have difficulty in making out pencil lines. In this case, you can scribble over the outline with white tailors' chalk instead, which can be easily seen. As tailors' chalk is more prone than pencil to smudge, do this very carefully.

Decide exactly where your tracing is to go and mark the point on the article. Try to avoid moving the tracing around too much, as the pencil will easily transfer on to the paintwork, making dirty marks.

Trim off the excess tracing paper around your design, and place the tracing paper, with the original outline face upwards, on your chosen surface.

Make sure your tracing is in the right position. Use a ruler to check the measurements if necessary. Then secure the tracing paper to the surface with masking tape or draughtsman's tape. Do not use any other sticky tape, as this may spoil the surface, and damage the paintwork.

With a ball-point pen or a hard pencil, draw over the original outlines of your design, pressing hard. This will transfer the outline of your image on to the surface. Check that you have transferred every outline.

Always trace the complete design on to your piece of furniture before you begin painting. This saves time, and gives you an idea of how the finished article will look.

If you make a mistake at all, you can wipe the pencil off quite easily, using a damp cloth.

Finally, remove any dirt and smudges, using a damp cloth and a little liquid scourer.

Painting the design

When painting, work in a logical progression – for example, from left to right, or from top to bottom. This has various advantages. First, you are less likely to smudge wet paint while you work, as you will always be moving away from the newly painted areas. Secondly, it ensures that you do not miss any areas out and always know exactly how much you have completed.

First, paint in all the flat, or main, areas of colour. You should apply one colour at a time, so that you paint the pink areas, then the blue areas, then the red areas of the design, and so on.

Let each colour dry thoroughly before beginning the next one, or you may smudge the existing outlines. The paints may take a couple of hours to dry. If you decide to add another colour before the previous one is dry, try not to paint areas bordering on the wet paint. This will reduce the risk of messy outlines.

Do not apply your paint too thickly. Its surface can easily be broken and the effect spoiled, if you touch it before it is dry. If the paint becomes too thick, thin it out with a little turpentine or white spirit.

If there are any white areas in your design, and you are painting on a white surface, it is better to leave these areas unpainted. There are so many different shades of white that you are unlikely to be able to match a white enamel paint exactly with the existing paintwork.

Let all the flat colours dry thoroughly before beginning the final stages of adding all the highlights.

Now add the finishing touches – a dark outline round the design, if you wish, or other small details, such as eyes, or buttons on a coat.

If you make a mistake or smudge the paint, wipe it away with a paper tissue, soaked in a little turpentine, or white spirit, after the paint has dried.

When you have finished, and all the paint is completely dry, carefully wipe off any remaining smudges with a damp cloth and a little liquid scourer.

SMALL AND BEAUTIFUL

Even the smallest room can be effectively decorated by thinking out what you want to do in advance. Plan your design carefully before you start, assessing any existing features to see whether or not you can utilize them to effect or deciding how you can alter them. Pre-planning not only enables you to produce the most effective and striking design – it will also save you time.

Giving such a room style and character need not be expensive either. Though I chose the penguin paper for this room, taking the motif as the basis for decorating furniture and fabrics could equally well be the answer, if, for instance, you find yourself stuck with an existing wallpaper

you cannot afford to change. Remember, in all that you do, you should be looking for ways of turning apparent disadvantages into advantages.

Here, the obvious disadvantage was the awkward angles between walls and ceiling. Rather than trying to avoid this, I decided to take the paper right on to the ceiling, thus giving a point to the angles, rather than apologizing for them. As the dado rail was already present, I tried to turn this to advantage as well by painting the lower half of the wall to break things up and make the overall effect more interesting. There was a practical reason for this, too – it is far easier to clean sticky fingermarks off paint than off wallpaper!

Mixing the motifs
To introduce a second animal element to the design, I added a hobby horse on a stand. By keeping to the blue, yellow and white colour scheme, I was able to incorporate the horse into the room.

Transforming a table top
Don't leave plain an area of white-painted wood when you could decorate it, given some care and imagination. I extended the motif of jumping penguins to the table, and ranged them around the top in a circle. They were varnished to protect them from scratches.

Maximizing space
As space was at a premium in this room, I pushed the cot against the wall. This meant the baby had more floorspace on which to crawl around, and could hold on to the bars of the cot while he was learning to walk.

PERSONAL TOUCHES

All children love to individualize their personal possessions and personalizing a table or chair with your child's name is one of the most appealing and effective ways of brightening up a playroom, bedroom or nursery.

Lettering need not only be used for personalizing furniture. You can create many exciting designs based on the alphabet, or numbers, for a young child's room. Make learning fun for your children, even from an early age.

Choosing your lettering

Your choice is enormous. You can use books or magazines, or go to your local art or graphic shop, which will have a vast range of lettering for you to look at. When you find something you like, you can have it reduced or enlarged to any size by a photocopying shop *(see p128)*, or you can do it yourself using a grid *(see pp60-1)*.

When choosing your lettering, remember that it should be clear and easily legible.

Equipment

Enamel model paints are ideal for decorating furniture *(see pp40-1)*. You will also need tracing paper as a palate for mixing the paint and a fine art brush. Prepare all your paint and equipment before beginning work *(see pp40-1)*.

The basic rules to follow when decorating any piece of furniture are always the same *(see pp40-1)*. Remember that for the best results any surface you are going to paint must be clean and smooth.

As easy as ABC
Using the alphabet as a decorative motif in the nursery and playroom makes learning fun. Combine it with other motifs – dot your i's with stars and flowers, perch birds on the bar of a t – or let your imagination run riot and transform s's into snakes and c's into crescent moons.

ABCDEF
GHIJKL
MNOPQRST
UVWXYZ

Tracing lettering

Draw a master line with a ruler on a long piece of tracing paper.

Positioning the tracing paper so that the bottom of the letter is resting on the master line, trace the first letter, drawing the straight lines with a ruler, and the rest freehand. Use either a fine pencil, or felt tip.

Move the tracing paper to the next letter. Leave a reasonable gap between the first and second letter. Use the master line to make sure that the letters follow a horizontal line.

Repeat the process for the third letter, and the fourth and so on, making sure that all the letters are equidistant, and following a perfectly horizontal line.

Turn the tracing paper over and scribble with a soft pencil over all the outlines. Do not scribble too liberally, as you may mark the existing paintwork.

It is vital that the lettering is positioned accurately. First, measure, and mark the point where you want to put the name, and draw in a guideline with a ruler. Put your tracing in roughly the right position. Check the measurements with a ruler, and a spirit level if necessary to check horizontal and vertical positioning, and adjust the tracing. Attach the tracing with masking tape or draughtsman's tape.

Using a ball-point pen, or sharp pencil, and pressing hard, trace round the outlines. Use a ruler for the straight lines, and draw the rest freehand.

Before you begin to paint, mix enough of your required colour to ensure the same shade and tone throughout.

Painting the lettering

It is quite difficult at first to achieve sharp clean outlines, so practise painting on a board before attempting to decorate a piece of furniture.

A comfortable working position is essential. Keep the surface that you are painting as horizontal as possible, so that you can steady your hand while you work.

To avoid smudging the paint, work from left to right if you are right-handed. If you are left-handed, work from right to left.

If you make a mistake, wait until the paint has completely dried, and then correct the fault using a paper tissue, soaked in a little turpentine or white spirit. Do not attempt to correct mistakes while the paint is still wet as it is much more likely to run.

Avoid the temptation to try to clarify the outlines of the letters after you have finished painting, as you will probably blur them more.

When you have completely finished, wipe off the pencil guidelines and any marks or smudges using a damp cloth and a little liquid scourer.

A sense of belonging

A name on anything from a pencil case to a table makes it special. Children feel great pride in seeing their own name on their belongings.

YOUR TODDLER

When I am grown to man's estate
I shall be very proud and great,
And tell the other girls and boys
Not to meddle with my toys.

Looking Forward

Robert Louis Stevenson
1850-1894

*Let your imagination run riot
when you plan the
decorative scheme of a
toddler's room.*

CONTENTS

WHAT EVERY TODDLER NEEDS

The years from two to five are the time of exploration. Children learn a great deal during these few years, and seem to do everything in top gear, being constantly on the move from morning to night. As a result, the room will become a playroom as well as a bedroom, and you must furnish and decorate it accordingly.

Changing from a cot to a bed

By the time your child reaches the age of two, you will probably want to move him or her from a cot to a bed. If you are expecting another baby, and need the cot for the new arrival, try to make the transition from cot to bed a couple of months before your new baby is born. Otherwise, your child may resent seeing the cot occupied by a new baby. This is a good reason why you should make the new bed as exciting as possible – your toddler will then feel pleased at the prospect of sleeping in it, and leaving the cot will not matter so much.

The great discovery for your child will be the ability to get out of bed without any help. This new-found freedom is wonderful, but you must ensure that it is not going to cause more problems than it solves by making sure that the room is as safe as you can make it (see pp24-5).

Making the room a playroom

Now that your child is older, he or she will need more furniture in the room, to convert it into a playroom. As children grow, the amount of toys they own appears to grow at a similar rate! You will want to tidy them away somewhere, and a toy chest is ideal. You can buy a chest, or make one yourself (see pp52-3). Use some child psychology by making the toy chest so attractive that your toddler enjoys using it!

A low chair and small table make an ideal place for a child to write, draw or paint, or hold make-believe tea parties with toys and friends. Children love furniture that has been specially decorated for them, with their favourite cartoon characters or their names (see pp40-1 and pp44-5). If you have an adult chair and table, you could cut down the legs to make them the right height for your child, before painting them to look as attractive and different as possible.

Toddlers love playing games in which they rush around, and they enjoy pulling carts. You can make a racing car trolley for your child following the instructions on the facing page.

Choosing the right floor-covering

Floor space is at a premium at this age, as children love to sit on the floor surrounded by simple jigsaws and puzzles, cars, books, bricks and all manner of toys and games. You must therefore plan the floor-covering very carefully, because it will have to take a lot of punishment. There is little point in going to the trouble of creating an exciting bedroom for your child if you are constantly worried about the carpet being ruined through accidents.

Coir matting and sisal will be too hard on bare knees and feet, and dirt can easily become engrained in the fibres. Cork flooring, however, is a much better option for a child's floor, since it is warm, comfortable underfoot, and washable. When your child gets older, you can cover the tiles with attractive, non-slip rugs.

It may be that a good-quality carpet has already been laid in your toddler's room, in which case you must protect it from undue damage. Buy some washable, hard-wearing rugs which you can place in strategic positions on the floor, to take most of the wear and tear.

Easy maintenance

Since toddlers are naturally untidy, you will want the room to be as easy to maintain as possible. Cut down on your workload as much as you can, by ensuring that all surfaces are wipeable, the floor can be cleaned, and nothing in the room is easily damaged. Make sure that any armchairs have loose covers, which you can remove and wash when they become dirty.

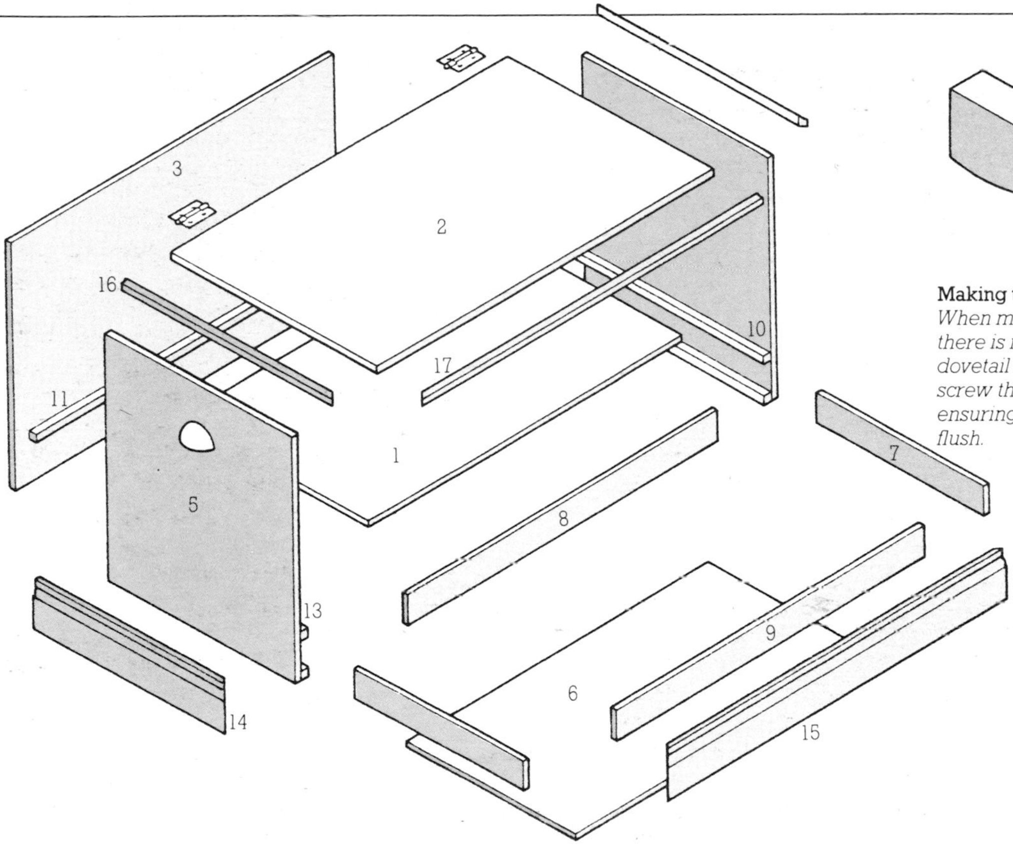

The magic toybox is both cheap and easy to make, and you can increase the proportions if you wish it to be larger.

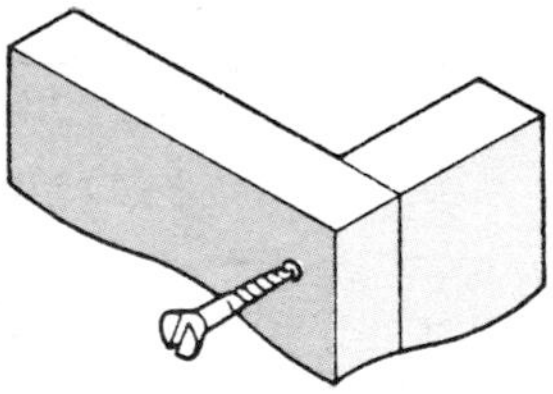

Making the joints
When making the toybox, there is no need to mitre or dovetail the joints. Glue and screw them together, ensuring that the ends are flush.

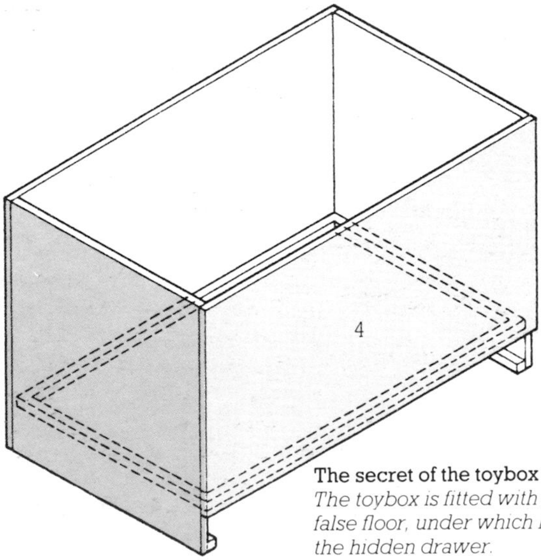

The secret of the toybox
The toybox is fitted with a false floor, under which lies the hidden drawer.

MATERIALS AND EQUIPMENT

Pieces

1 Floor	1	400 x 676 x 12mm	(16 x 27 x ½in)
2 Lid	1	400 x 700 x 12mm	(16 x 28 x ½in)
3 Back	1	700 x 460 x 12mm	(28 x 18⅖ x ½in)
4 Front	1	700 x 385 x 12mm	(28 x 15⅖ x ½in)
5 Sides	2	400 x 460 x 12mm	(16 x 18⅖ x ½in)
6 Drawer floor	1	676 x 375 x 12mm	(27 x 15 x ½in)
7 Drawer sides	2	375 x 54 x 12mm	(15 x 2⅙ x ½in)
8 Drawer back	1	676 x 54 x 12mm	(27 x 2⅙ x ½in)
9 Drawer front	1	700 x 54 x 12mm	28 x 2⅙ x ½in)
10 Side runners	2	400 x 15 x 15mm	16 x ⅗ x ⅗in)
11 Back runner	1	644 x 15 x 15mm	(25¾ x ⅗ x ⅗in)
12 Front runner	1	644 x 15 x 15mm	(25¾ x ⅗ x ⅗in)
13 Floor support	1	400 x 15 x 15mm	(16 x ⅗ x ⅗in)
14 Side mouldings	2	424 x 80 x 15mm	(17 x 3⅕ x ⅗in)
15 Drawer mouldings	1	700 x 80 x 15mm	(28 x 3⅕ x ⅗in)
16 Side lid mouldings	2	452 x 32 x 15mm	(18 1/16 x 1¼ x ⅗in)
17 Front lid moulding	1	754 x 32 x 15mm	(30⅙ x 1¼ x ⅗in)

Attachments

Hinges	2	piano, butt or cranked
Handles	2	Brass
Knobs	4	Wooden

Equipment

Saw, hammer, screwdriver, drill, countersink bit, screws, panel pins, wood glue, pencil for marking, ruler, set square, sandpaper and paint

A TOUCH OF CLASS

You can never tell what children will like – many children would hate this room, but it was just what Rasha, the little girl in the picture, wanted. What I aimed to do was to take into account her taste, keeping the sophisticated look of the original room, while adding a few touches to make it less forbidding and adult-like. I achieved this simply through the use of paint and colour.

Having chosen a wallpaper with a small pink dot pattern, I decided to paint the original dark moulding pink as well to lighten the effect. The pink pattern is also picked out in the curtains – in fact, the child-sized sofa and chair is also covered with the same fabric.

The painted motifs on the furniture also stemmed from the fabric design. The motifs were scaled up, transferred on to the furniture and then coloured in *(see pp40-1)*. On the doors, I picked out the moulding and painted little squirrels in the panels, again to create a contrasting lightness of touch.

Providing privacy
Children need privacy as much as adults. If your child's bedroom is overlooked, hanging up net curtains is one answer to this. The frill at the bottom of these net curtains matches the frilled pelmet of the main curtains, and their whiteness blends in well with the crisp, classic feel of the room.

Creating a seating area
If your child has the same sophisticated tastes as Rasha, give him or her a small sofa. Keep the room suitable for a child by adding a child-sized table and matching chairs.

Keep the room friendly
Large rooms can look very barren, so arrange the furniture in the room to overcome the problem. Toys can also be used to effectively fill up the space, and need not necessarily make the room look untidy!

Matching wastepaper bin
Remember to incorporate every item in the room into your design scheme in some way or other. Here, I painted a simple wooden wastepaper bin with the same motif that I used on the door.

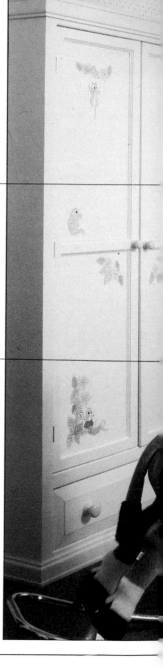

THE WENDY HOUSE

Children love having their very own home. This Wendy house is sturdy and hardwearing, and, painted imaginatively, will provide hours of enjoyment. The floor is chipboard, the roof plywood, and the frame and balustrade are pine.

Preparing the basic structure

With a pencil and ruler, measure and mark out all the pieces for the house. Saw them out. On the larger half of the roof (2), fix battens (7) along both long sides, 12mm (½in) from one edge, and 100mm (4in) from the other with panel pins. Leave a 50-mm (2-in) gap at either end. On the smaller half of the roof (1), fix the other roof support batten (7) 100mm (4in) from the edge in the same way, but this time only along one side (see diagram).

The walls of the Wendy house and balustrades should be positioned 50mm (2in) from the edges of the floor. Draw a floor plan as shown. Then mark the positions of the floor support battens (6) on the underside of the floor (see diagram). Countersink holes in the floor for the screws, using a drill and countersink bit. Screw the floor support battens in place.

Saw the tops of the side supports (8) at an angle of 45°, and sand them smooth. Countersink holes for the screws down the front and back edges of the sides (4). Screw side supports to the inside of the front and back edges of the sides. Make sure the side supports are flush with the edges. Using a jig saw, cut the windows in the sides.

Putting the house together

Using wood glue and panel pins, fix the wall battens (12) to the bottom edges of the sides (4). Countersink holes for the screws through the wall battens. Hold the sides in position and fix them in place by glueing and screwing the wall battens to the floor. Countersink holes down the outside edges of the back of the house (3) and screw the back in place.

Countersink holes for the screws along the

A home of their own
A Wendy house is a home from home for your children,

where they can play at being grown-up and entertain their friends to tea.

batten-less edge of the larger half of the roof (2). Fit both halves of the roof in place (see diagram). Fix the roof securely with glue and screws.

The balustrade and windows

With a pencil and ruler, mark the positions of the balustrade posts (10) on the upper and lower rails (9) of the balustrades. Drill holes at these points and fix the posts in place to the rails with wood glue. Make sure that each post fits squarely to the rails at both ends. Countersink holes for screws in the remaining two side support posts (8) and screw them to the balustrades. Countersink holes for the screws in the bottom rail of the balustrade and fix the bottom rail of the balustrade to the floor with wood glue and screws.

Using a jig saw, cut heart-shaped holes in the shutters (11) if you wish. Fix them with panel pins on either side of the window. Make sure that the edges of the shutters are flush with the window.

The finishing touches

Fill any holes with proprietary filler, and sand the house smooth. Paint the Wendy house as you wish – turn it into an Elizabethan timbered cottage, or an alpine hut.

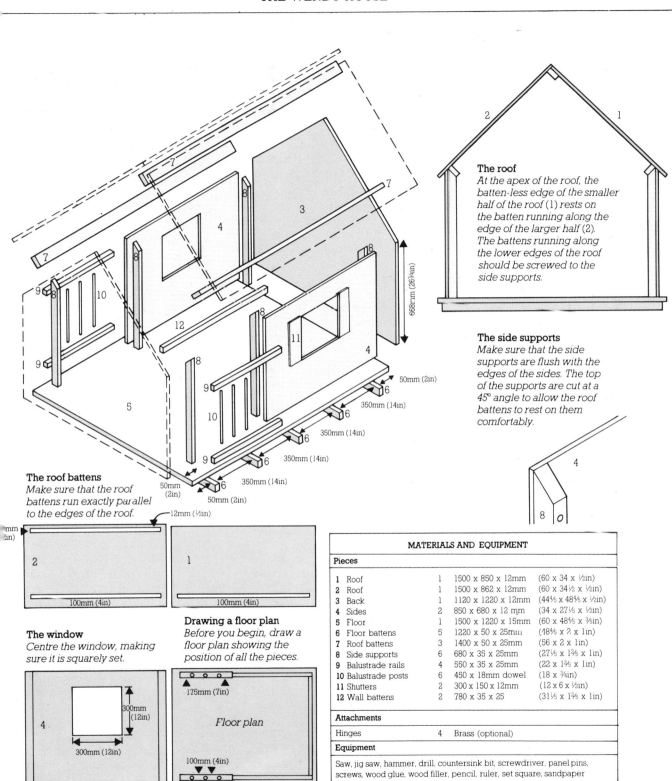

The roof
At the apex of the roof, the batten-less edge of the smaller half of the roof (1) rests on the batten running along the edge of the larger half (2). The battens running along the lower edges of the roof should be screwed to the side supports.

The side supports
Make sure that the side supports are flush with the edges of the sides. The top of the supports are cut at a 45° angle to allow the roof battens to rest on them comfortably.

The roof battens
Make sure that the roof battens run exactly parallel to the edges of the roof.

The window
Centre the window, making sure it is squarely set.

Drawing a floor plan
Before you begin, draw a floor plan showing the position of all the pieces.

MATERIALS AND EQUIPMENT			
Pieces			
1 Roof	1	1500 x 850 x 12mm	(60 x 34 x ½in)
2 Roof	1	1500 x 862 x 12mm	(60 x 34½ x ½in)
3 Back	1	1120 x 1220 x 12mm	(44⅘ x 48⅘ x ½in)
4 Sides	2	850 x 680 x 12 mm	(34 x 27⅕ x ½in)
5 Floor	1	1500 x 1220 x 15mm	(60 x 48⅘ x ⅗in)
6 Floor battens	5	1220 x 50 x 25mm	(18⅘ x 2 x 1in)
7 Roof battens	3	1400 x 50 x 25mm	(56 x 2 x 1in)
8 Side supports	6	680 x 35 x 25mm	(27⅕ x 1⅖ x 1in)
9 Balustrade rails	4	550 x 35 x 25mm	(22 x 1⅖ x 1in)
10 Balustrade posts	6	450 x 18mm dowel	(18 x ¾in)
11 Shutters	2	300 x 150 x 12mm	(12 x 6 x ½in)
12 Wall battens	2	780 x 35 x 25	(31⅕ x 1⅖ x 1in)
Attachments			
Hinges	4	Brass (optional)	
Equipment			
Saw, jig saw, hammer, drill, countersink bit, screwdriver, panel pins, screws, wood glue, wood filler, pencil, ruler, set square, sandpaper			

FAIRY TALE FANTASY

Compare this with the preceding room, and you will see exactly what I mean about differing tastes! Here, the room obviously needed a single dramatic decorative image to overcome the problems posed by a vast expanse of wall. The easiest way of doing this was to paint a mural. So, Snow White and the Seven Dwarves met Humpty Dumpty!

Many professionals prefer to create murals freehand, but don't let this put you off. You could achieve the same effect by simply tracing off the design you want from a children's book *(see p128)* on to a grid, which you can then use as the basis for a scaled-up master drawing on the wall *(see pp60-1).*

Making a mural
Remember that most children love completeness, so the more you can make your mural tell a story, the more satisfactory it will be for them. You can also be as ambitious and elaborate, or as simple and unsophisticated, as you choose. Humpty Dumpty, for instance, is relatively easy to draw and you could well take his story as the major dominant feature of your mural.

Trompe l'oeil
You can use a child's favourite nursery rhyme or story in any number of ways. In this room, I extended the lines of the elegant fireplace to create a trompe l'oeil clock, taking Hickory Dickory Dock as my theme. As well as providing an interest to an otherwise blank wall, this linked up with the mural on the other side of the room.

Providing a playpen
Given enough toys, a toddler will sit happily in a playpen. The nearby armchair is large enough for an adult to sit in and chat to the child.

Choosing a carpet
If you want to fit a carpet in your toddler's room, choose one in a colour that won't show the dirt too much. A light brown shade, such as the one shown here, is ideal. Ensure that it is hard-wearing and will be easy to clean – something that is bound to be necessary.

PAINTING A MURAL

Murals are an unusual and exciting way of turning even the most boring of rooms into somewhere special: and painting a mural is much easier than many people think. A blank wall can suddenly become the window on to a woodland scene, or intergalactic battle. Murals do not necessarily have to be large and to dominate an entire room – even small murals can be equally effective if carefully positioned. With just a little forethought, and the mastery of a few basic techniques, successful murals are within everyone's reach, although painting a mural can be time-consuming.

Choosing a design
You can choose any design or picture from any source. Try to envisage what your picture or design will look like, enlarged several times to wall size, and think carefully about positioning your mural. Where will it be at its most effective?

Paints and painting equipment
You can use almost any paint for murals – emulsions, resin-based paints, oils and acrylics are all suitable. You will also need a variety of brushes. For mixing colours, jam jars, or tin foil dishes for larger brushes, are ideal. Always mix enough paint before you begin to cover all the areas of that colour on the mural. If you have to remix a colour, you may have problems matching it to the original shade.

Preparing to paint
Wash the wall or repaint it if necessary. Move, or cover furniture in danger of being splashed with paint while you are at work and protect the adjacent floor area with plastic, newspaper or cloth. Make sure you have something secure to stand on to reach the upper part of the wall. A sturdy stepladder is ideal. You must be able to reach every part of the wall quite comfortably and safely – you should never have to stretch.

Painting the mural
Draw the complete outline of your mural on the wall. Stand back from it, and make sure it is what you want before you start begin painting.

Begin by filling in all the larger, flat expanses of colour. Use the paler colours first. Complete all the areas of one colour at a time. Remember to work methodically. It is best to work from the top to the bottom of the mural, as this means the minimum fuss with stepladders, and you will not be leaning over wet paint. Allow the paint to dry thoroughly. The time this takes will depend on the type of paint you are using.

Take your second colour and complete all the appropriate areas. Allow to dry, then apply the third colour, and so on, until the main areas of colour are all painted. Add the final small details, and a fine outline with black paint, or with a black spirit-type felt tip pen if you wish, which is easier, if a little less effective. When the mural is dry, paint it with matt varnish to protect it.

Correcting mistakes
If you make a mistake at any time, allow the paint to dry before attempting to correct it, as you may only cause the rest of the paint to run or smear. Correct mistakes with a rag, or paper tissue, soaked in a little turpentine or white spirit. Also remember that mistakes can be painted out.

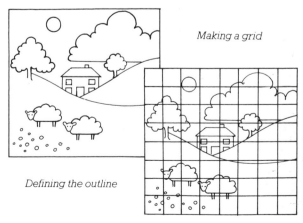

Making a grid

Defining the outline

Simple and effective

Too many pictures and posters can make a room look muddled. Keep the pictures simple, and give them a linking theme, such as the same colour.

Making use of space

In a small room there may not be enough space for all the conventional pieces of bedroom furniture. In this room, a gaily decorated chest of drawers doubles up as a bedside table. The painted surface means that spilled drinks will not spoil the wood, and the bedside light is within reach if the child wakes up in the middle of the night from a nightmare.

PC Plod

The beauty of using figures such as these in your decorative scheme is that their outlines are very simple. It is therefore quite easy to trace them and then transfer them on to a wall, prior to painting a mural.

MAKING A FORT

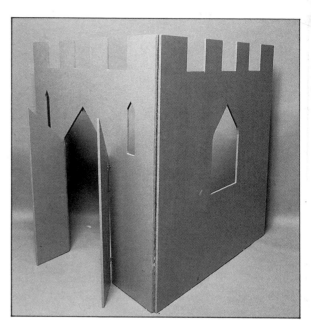

Once more unto the breach *fun scaling the ramparts or*
Children can have hours of *fighting off attackers.*

A simple and sturdy fort, which is L-shaped and has two sides, can be fitted neatly into the corner of a room. It gives every child the chance to be king or queen of the castle and provides the refuge all children need at times from the adult world. The fort is made of plywood, so that it is both strong and quite light.

The windows and ramparts

Cut out the front *(1)* and side *(2)* walls with a saw. With a pencil, mark out the ramparts and windows on both front and side walls as shown. Check that all the angles of the ramparts are square, using a set square. The window in the side wall should be centred, as shown, 450mm (18in) from the base. Check that it is squarely positioned. Position the windows on the front wall where you like, but make sure that they are arranged symmetrically. Saw out the ramparts, and cut out the windows with a jig saw.

Making and fitting the door

With a pencil, mark out the doorway in the front wall as shown. Saw out the doorway in the front wall with great care – the cut-out is to become the door itself.

Saw the door lengthways in half, and sand down the edges. Sand down the edges of the doorway. Attach the doors with hinges to the outside of the doorway, checking that the doors will open and close easily. To prevent the door from opening inwards, fix a piece of plywood with panel pins about 50mm (2in) below the top of the doorway to act as a door stop.

Completing the fort

You can fix the front and side of the fort together with ordinary hinges, but piano hinges provide the strongest and most resilient join. If you cannot buy the piano hinge already cut, cut it to length yourself with a hack saw. With the piano hinge, attach the front and side walls of the fort together.

If the fort is to be fixed permanently against walls with skirting boards, cut out a small recess from the base of each corner of the fort to allow the edge of the wall to fit snugly against the wall.

Sand the whole structure smooth and make sure that the edges are splinter-free and that there are no sharp corners. Paint the fort in an appropriate colour. Our fort is just painted grey but you can paint in the details of the stonework and the solid oak of the doors and make your castle seem as real as possible, so that, once inside, any defender would feel safe under siege. There are other decorative ideas you could use. You may like to add some trails of ivy or bunches of moss lying between the stones; or you could drape some heraldic banners or flags from the ramparts.

Fixing the fort in position

If the fort is to stay in one room permanently, you can fix it in place with standard right-angled metal brackets. Screw two brackets to the outer edges of each wall of the fort. Make sure they are squarely set, using a set square. Screw the brackets firmly to the walls. Before doing so, make sure that the outside edges of the fort stand flush against the walls.

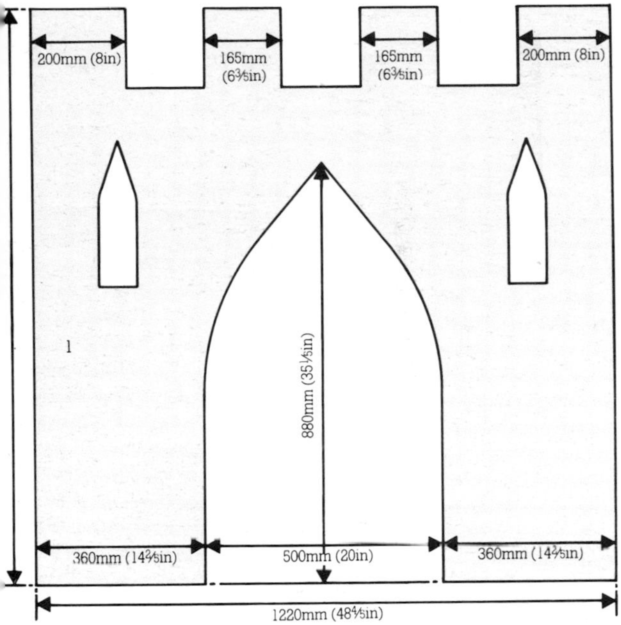
200mm (8in)
165mm (6⅗in)
165mm (6⅗in)
200mm (8in)
1
880mm (35⅕in)
360mm (14⅖in)
500mm (20in)
360mm (14⅖in)
1220mm (48⅘in)
1

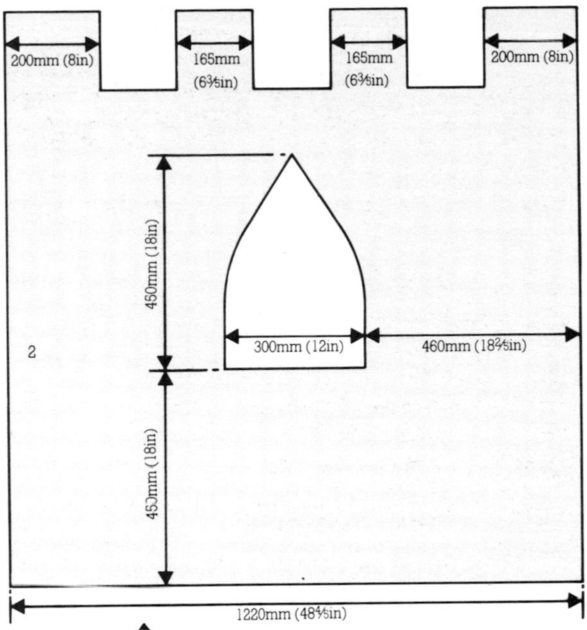
200mm (8in)
165mm (6⅗in)
165mm (6⅗in)
200mm (8in)
450mm (18in)
2
300mm (12in)
460mm (18⅘in)
453mm (18in)
1220mm (48⅘in)

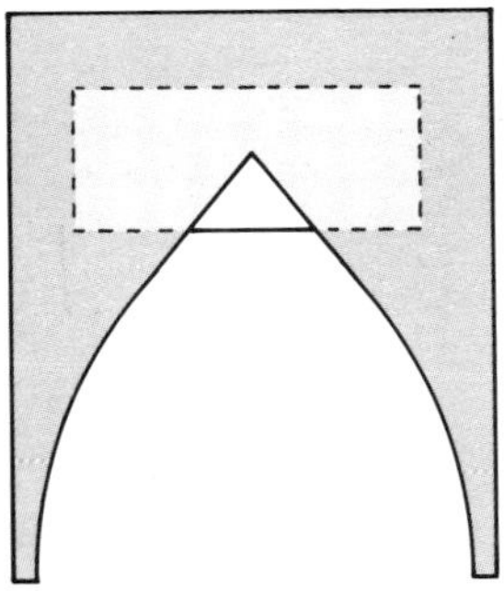

Making a door stop
To prevent the door from opening inwards, pin a small rectangle of plywood across the doorway, 50mm (2in) below the top of the door.

Positioning the fort
If the fort is to stay permanently in one room, it can be attached to the wall with brackets. If necessary cut spaces for the skirting boards in either corner of the fort.

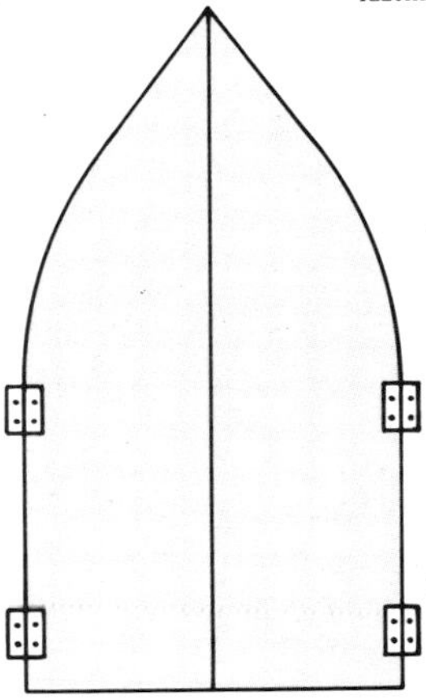

Making the door
The two halves of the door should be perfectly symmetrical, and should open and close together smoothly. Check the doors fit snugly in place before trying to hinge them. If they stick at all, sand down the edges a little more.

Make sure that the door is large enough for your child. If you think it is rather small, make it larger.

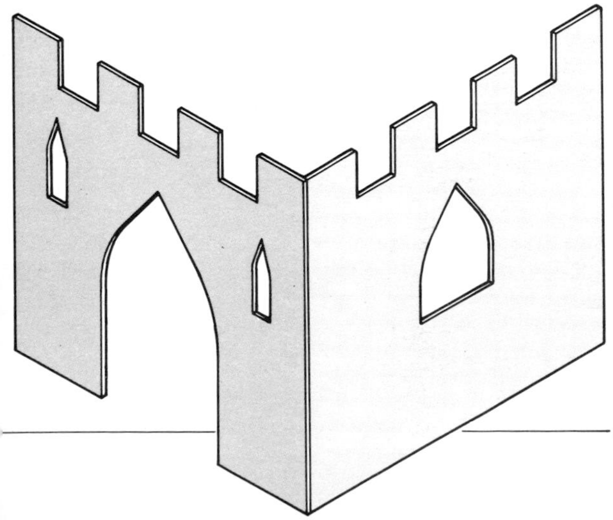

MATERIALS AND EQUIPMENT			
Pieces			
1 Front wall	1	1220 x 1220 x 12mm	(48⅘ x 48⅘ x ½in)
2 Side wall	1	1220 x 1220 x 12mm	(48⅘ x 48⅘ x ½in)
Attachments			
Hinge	1	piano, 1200mm (48in)	
Brackets	4	Metal	
Equipment			
Saw, jig saw, metal hack saw, screwdriver, screws, panel pins, sandpaper, paint, pencil for marking, ruler, set square			

STARTING SCHOOL

A child should always say what's true,
And speak when he is spoken to,
And behave mannerly at table:
At least as far as he is able.

Whole Duty of Children

Robert Louis Stevenson
1850-1894

Walls can be used to display a complete fantasy land, inspired in this case by Brambly Hedge.

CONTENTS

WHAT EVERY SCHOOLCHILD NEEDS

The day your child starts school will be a momentous one for both of you. At first, there will still be a large proportion of the day when your child will be at home, because he or she will go to school in the mornings only.

When young children are at home, they love to do all the things that they do at school. You should therefore design a young schoolchild's room with these interests in mind, aiming to achieve a good balance between encouraging your child to learn and to play. If you do not have a separate playroom, your child's bedroom will become the place in which he or she will sleep, play and work, and you must design it as such.

Tidying up

You will now need a greater amount of storage space to accommodate the ever-increasing number of possessions your child is accumulating.

If you already have fitted cupboards in the room you might be able to add some more shelves to increase your storage space. It may be that there is an alcove in the room in which you could build a fitted cupboard (see pp72-3). A toy chest is an ideal receptacle for a child's clutter (see pp52-3). You can make it more attractive by painting on his or her name, or decorating it with motifs taken from the design of the room. If the room is small, and space is at a premium, you could keep the toys and games in a large sliding drawer which you have made to fit beneath the bed. This will maximize the floor space on which your child can play.

Books and bookshelves

By now, your child should be discovering the exciting world of books. As well as being a source of pleasure, and an important part of your child's education, they add character to any room.

I firmly believe in teaching young children that books should be well looked after – in other words, be put away properly! The most obvious way of doing this is to give your child a set of personalized bookshelves. You can make your own (see pp76-7), and decorate them to match the design of the room. If you fix the shelves to the wall at a height your child can reach, he or she will be able to take the books out and replace them when necessary. Books will only get torn if they are thrown into a toy box.

Hanging a blackboard

A wall blackboard can add excitement to a room, and you can decorate it in any way you like to make it look attractive. If you make your own (see pp80-1), you will be able to cut the board out into a special shape, taken from a motif you are using elsewhere in the room. Alternatively, you could keep the shape of the blackboard simple, but paint a design on it, such as a cartoon character, animal, aeroplane or train.

Giving your child a blackboard will serve two purposes. As well as being an interesting focal point of the room, it will encourage your child to read and write. He or she can pretend to be a teacher at school, and give lessons to toys and younger brothers and sisters, or friends.

Increasing the seating

Children of this age enjoy playing on the floor, although they will also enjoy sitting at their own tables to play games or paint. Provide your child with enough floor space, therefore, so that he or she does not feel constricted.

If you want to increase the amount of seating in the room, buy an inexpensive bean bag or make a large floor cushion (see facing page). Cover the floor cushion with a hard-wearing fabric, such as heavy-duty cotton, or canvas. Fill it with foam chips, kapok or feathers. You can stuff a bean bag with polystyrene granules. For scatter cushions, choose any soft furnishing or dressmaking fabric for the cover, and fill them with feathers, kapok or foam chips. Remember you can use a patterned fabric or a plain one, and then decorate it, using an appliqué design (see pp104-5) or painting the fabric (see pp84-5).

Making the cushion pad

Use a plain light cotton material. If you intend to fill the cushions with feathers, the material should be feather-proof. Measure and mark the two squares or rectangles for the front and back of the cushion pad. Allow for a seam of 16mm (⅝in) on each side. Cut the rectangles/squares out.

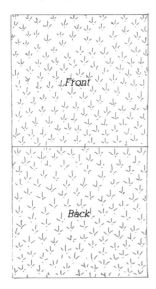

The front and back sides of the cushion pad should be the same shape and size. Measure them carefully on the fabric with a ruler and mark with tailors' chalk. Then cut them out with dressmaking scissors.

Pin the front and back of the cushion pad right sides together. Machine along three sides. Turn the cushion right sides out. Fill the cushion pad with your selected filling until it feels firm. Pin the two sides of the opening together, tack and then machine.

Making a cushion cover

Mark, measure and cut two more rectangles or squares of your chosen cover fabric, the same size as those you used for the cushion itself. If your cushion is feather-filled, cut the fabric for the cover about 12mm (½in) smaller than the size you used for the actual cushion. This gives the cushion a firm finish. Machine along three sides. Turn the cover right sides out.

Put a fringe, a ruffle,

piping, or cord in an attractive colour around the edge of the cushion, and stitch it in place. Alternatively appliqué or paint a design.

Close the opening in the cover with a zip, positioning it so that the teeth are covered by the overlap of the two edges of the front and back of the cushion as they meet. Pin, tack and machine the zip in place, using a zipper foot.

Check that the cover fits well – the covered cushion should have a firm, neat outline.

Cut the corners of the fabric, and cut out small triangle shapes around the edge of the seams. This allows the seams to lie flat and gives a neat finish to the cushion.

PICNIC WITH TOAD

In common with all children, yours will have their own particular favourite stories and story-book characters; I know that mine do! Creating the atmosphere of Kenneth Grahame's river bank, immortalized in *The Wind in the Willows*, was not easy – especially since most children have their own vision of Mole, Rat and Toad – so I went back to the original illustrations for inspiration. Because of the mural's complicated design – especially when it came down to points of detail – and the extremely delicate nature of the colours, I applied a base coat of eggshell first of all. This is the best paint to use as a base for any complex mural design.

When you create a mural like this, you should start with the background, work up the main features and only then start picking out the details *(see pp60-1)*. This means painting the mural in stages. As always, consider how you can use a motif elsewhere in the room – Toad himself makes a striking toy box feature, while I even hand-painted him on to the lampshade *(see pp84-5)*.

If space and ability allow, you could take the theme further than this. You might decide, for instance, to create some more paintings to show Toad's further adventures – remember that such designs can be an invaluable learning tool.

Lampshades
Even a lampshade can be incorporated into your design. For example, you can choose a lamp base and shade in a colour to match the design of the room. However, if you can't find something suitable, you can create one yourself. Buy a paper or fabric shade, or a kit with which you can make your own. Using fabric paints, decorate the shade with a motif that appears elsewhere in the room. You can either do this freehand or with a tracing.

Protecting a mural
Once you have finished painting a mural, you should protect it against wear and tear with a coat of matt polyurethane varnish. This will also mean it is washable – an important consideration in a child's room! Remember, too, that a clear varnish will also bring out the colours in a mural.

Bright bed linen
Instead of trying to buy a set of bed linen that matches your design scheme, you can make your own. Paint a suitable motif directly on to a duvet or bedspread, using fabric paints, or even sew on an appliqué.

Storage space
Toys are very important to children of all ages. An attractive way of storing them is in a toy box, which you can decorate with your child's name, or a motif taken from the room.

A FITTED CUPBOARD

This is a fitted cupboard you can adapt to fit any recess or alcove, provided that the walls are straight. The shelves and top are made of melamine-faced chipboard, the door frame of pine, the battens of plywood, and the ready-made doors can be bought from any d-i-y shop. They are available in a wide variety of sizes.

Deciding the size

Measure the width and height of the recess. The width gives you the length of the top and bottom of the door frame (4) and the height gives you the length of the sides of the door frame (5). Buy a size of doors (1) closest to the size of your recess, allowing at least 45mm (1⅜in) on each side for the door frame. The actual width of the frame should be equal to the distance of the gap between the doors and the walls of the recess. Also, allow another 100mm (4in) at the bottom of the cupboard for the false plinth (8).

Measure the width and depth of the recess to give you the width and depth of the shelves (3). The top of the cupboard (2) should be the same width as the shelves, but add an extra 20mm (⅘in) for the overlap, and another 25mm (1in) to allow for the thickness of the door frame. The back battens for the shelves (6) should be 50mm (2in) shorter than the length of the shelves and the side battens 50mm (2in) shorter than the width of the shelves. The plinth (8) should be as wide as the recess and 100mm (4in) high.

Mark all the shelf positions with a pencil and ruler. Mark out all the pieces and saw them out. You will need two side battens (7) and one back batten (6) for each shelf and the same for the top (2).

Making the cupboard

Countersink holes for the screws along the length of all the battens, using a drill and countersink bit. Fit the battens for the back of the recess, leaving a 25-mm (1-in) gap at either end. Screw

Hidden treasures
You need somewhere to store all the books and toys when the day's games are all over. Filling a recess with a fitted cupboard can be the perfect answer.

them in place and then fit the battens to the sides of the recess in the same way, leaving a 50-mm (2-in) gap at the front ends. Fix the shelves (3) on top of the battens with panel pins.

The door frame should be the same thickness as the door itself. Cut halved joints at the end of each piece of the frame (see diagram). Countersink holes for the screws in the joints, and fix the frame together with wood glue and screws. Check the joints are square with a set square.

Fit the frame on to the front of the shelves. Make sure it is flush with the shelves, and squarely set, and then screw it to the shelf battens. Fit the doors in the frame, and attach them to the frame with hinges.

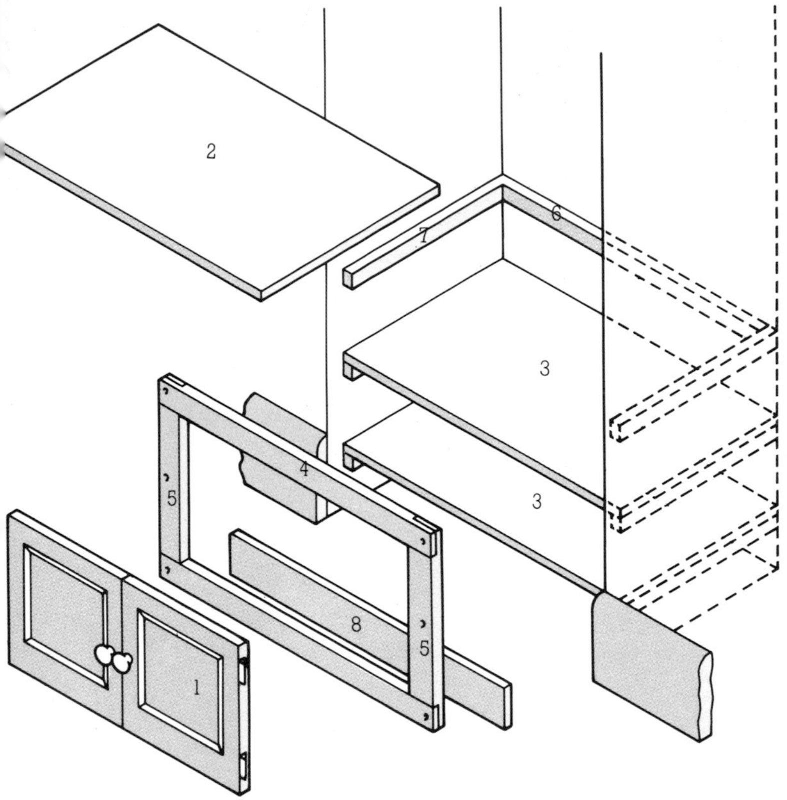

Fix the top *(2)* on top of the support battens with glue and panel pins. Slip the false plinth *(8)* under the cupboard. Fix it in place with panel pins.

The finishing touches

Sand the cupboard smooth and paint it with a coat of primer. Allow this to dry and then paint it with a top coat.

MATERIALS AND EQUIPMENT			
Pieces			
1 Doors	2	570 x 495 x 25mm	(22⅘ x 19⅘ x 1in)
2 Top	1	1080 x 420 x 12mm	(43⅕ x 16⅘ x ½in)
3 Shelves	2	1080 x 400 x 12mm	(43⅕ x 16 x½in
4 Top and bottom frames	2	1080 x 45 x 25mm	(43⅕ x 1⅘ x 1in)
5 Side frames	2	660 x 45 x 25mm	(26⅖ x 1⅘ x 1in)
6 Back shelf battens	3	1030 x 30 x 25mm	(41⅕ x 1in)
7 Side shelf battens	6	350 x 30 x 25mm	(14 x 1⅕ x 1in)
8 False plinth	1	1080 x 100 x 12mm	(43⅕ x 4 x ½in)
Attachments			
Hinges	4	Brass	
Equipment			
Screwdriver, saw, drill, countersink bit, hammer, screws, panel pins, wood glue, pencil for marking, ruler, sandpaper, primer, paint			

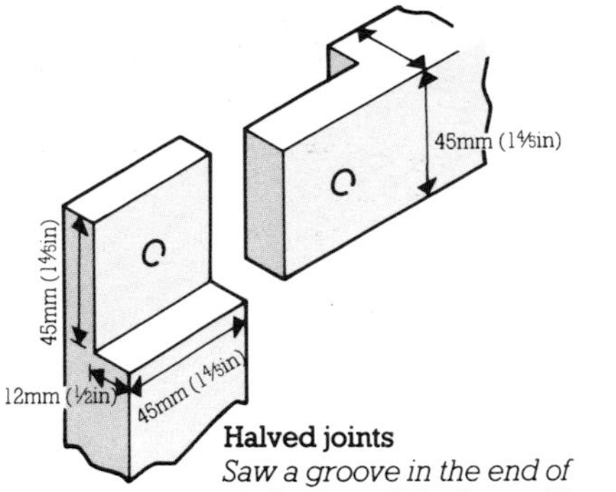

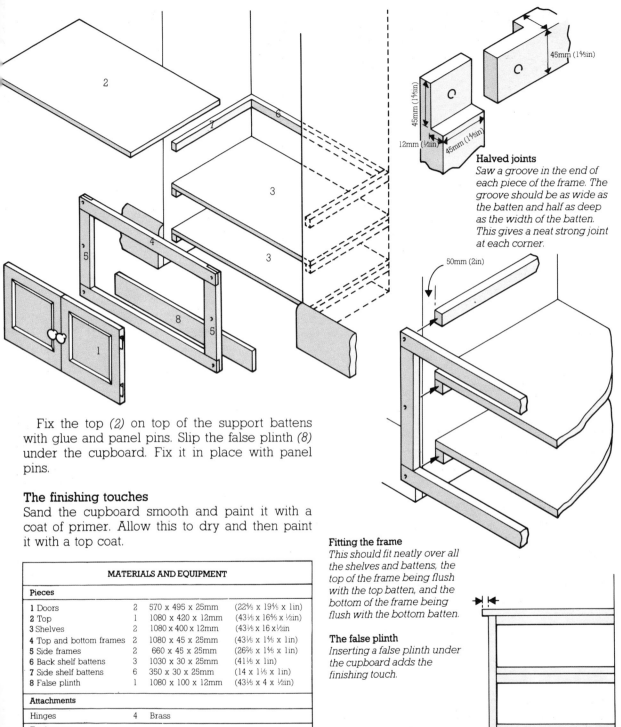

Halved joints
Saw a groove in the end of each piece of the frame. The groove should be as wide as the batten and half as deep as the width of the batten. This gives a neat strong joint at each corner.

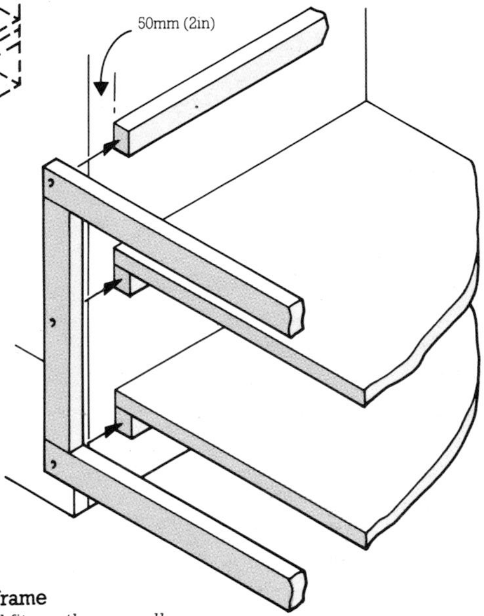

Fitting the frame
This should fit neatly over all the shelves and battens, the top of the frame being flush with the top batten, and the bottom of the frame being flush with the bottom batten.

The false plinth
Inserting a false plinth under the cupboard adds the finishing touch.

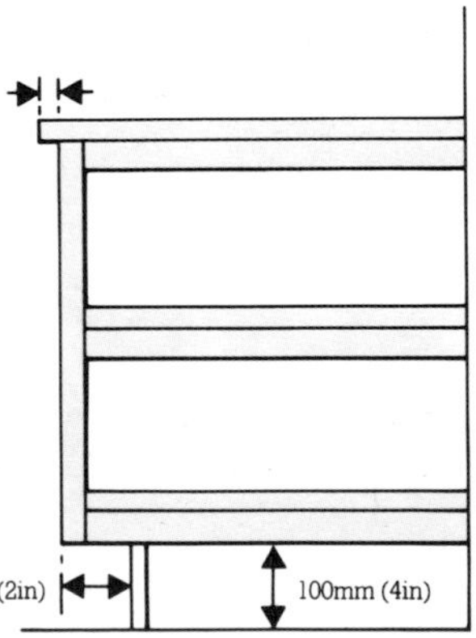

NB The measurements given here will make a fitted cupboard 772mm x 1080mm (31 x 43⅕in)

ROOM WITH A VIEW

In common with many parents, the problems of space may force you to 'double up' your children, rather than giving each one a room of their own. If this is the case, you can still add that important touch of individuality – and avoid squabbles and charges of favouritism – by deliberately planning a dual style right from the start.

You may face other practical problems as well – all of which you should try to resolve, rather than ignore. Suppose, for instance, that the room is windowless. In such a case, you could create a realistic painted window as a dramatic *trompe l'oeil (see pp92-3)*, and provide the view your children would like to see if they could. In the main picture here, even the cat and potted plant are all part of the effect! Or, if you are confronted by mass-market fitted cupboards and furniture in glaring white, use this as a basis to create an all-embracing mural *(see pp60-1)*, like the dramatic spacescape shown here.

Intergalactic interior
Don't be confined by this century when your child could be flung firmly into the space age. This mural completely dominates the room, as it is continued over the furniture and fittings, such as the picture rail and shelves. When decorating a room like this, try to look at everyday objects in a new way. A wooden bed head, for example, could be painted silver, to make it look more futuristic.

Mural by Anna de Polnay

Keep it simple
If you have as strong a feature as this trompe l'oeil *in a room, don't allow the rest of your design to compete with it. Instead, plan the room around it, and accentuate it in that way.*

Bringing a design to life
It is the little details that count and breathe life into a design scheme. The addition of the cat sitting on the windowsill looking out into the garden is the perfect finishing touch to this trompe l'oeil.

Varying patterns
Decorations on pieces of furniture do not always have to be symmetrically positioned, so long as finished design is kept in mind. Here, the balloons float from the bottom left-hand corner of the drawers to the top right-hand corner, and a tiny balloon and a miniature kite balance the design in the other corners.

SIMPLE STORAGE

Storage space in the bedroom or playroom is always needed. There are two versions of this multi-purpose storage unit. Standing upright it becomes a bookcase, on its side it becomes a bedside table.

Making the bookcase

With a pencil and ruler mark out all the pieces for the bookcase *(1, 2, 3 and 4)* and saw them out. Mark out the positions of the joints *(see diagram)*. Cut the grooves, either with a router, or by sawing down the sides of the groove, and chiselling out the centre.

If you do not wish to make grooved joints, the shelves can be fixed in place with wood glue and pins. In this case, you must reduce the length of each shelf by 20mm (⅘in) to take the absence of the grooves into account.

Fix the bottom two shelves *(2)* and the central divider *(4)* together with wood glue and panel pins. Check that the joints are firm and square, using a set square. Fix the small shelf *(3)* to the central divider *(4)* with wood glue and panel pins. Make sure that the small shelf is square.

Bring in the two sides of the bookcase to fit round the central assembly you have made. Checking carefully that the joints are all square, join the sides to the shelves with wood glue and panel pins.

Sand the bookcase smooth. Paint the bookcase with a coat of primer. Allow this to dry and then apply a coat of gloss paint.

Making the bedside table

The bedside table is assembled in exactly the same way as the bookcase, but what were the sides of the bookcase *(1)* become the top and bottom of the bedside table. When you have finished assembling the bedside table, sand the corners of the top and bottom until they are rounded. Then make the feet by screwing wooden door knobs to each of the bottom corners.

The simple storage unit
The ideal way to keep the bedroom tidy, the shelves of the storage unit have been designed to hold books, records, sketch pads, tapes or files.

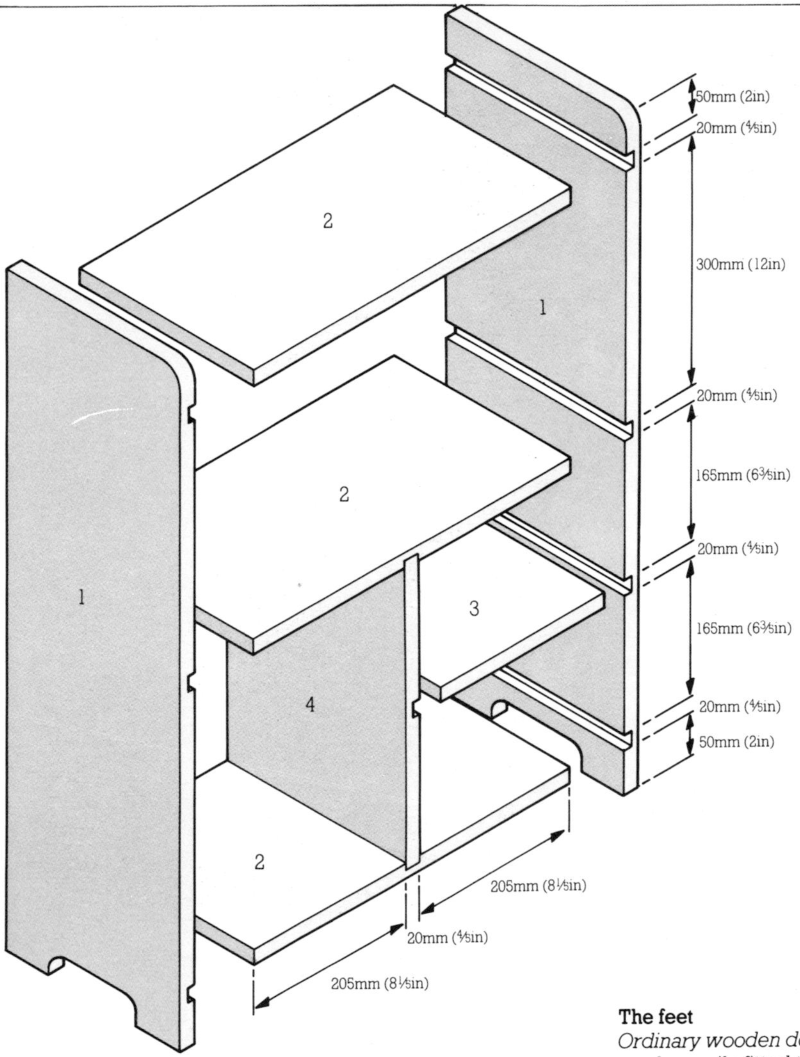
50mm (2in)
20mm (4/5in)
300mm (12in)
20mm (4/5in)
165mm (6 3/5in)
20mm (4/5in)
165mm (6 3/5in)
20mm (4/5in)
50mm (2in)
2
1
2
1
3
4
2
205mm (8 1/5in)
20mm (4/5in)
205mm (8 1/5in)

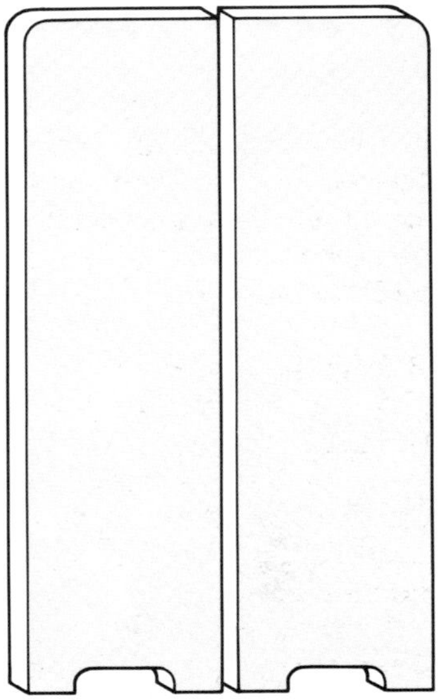

The recessed sides
Cutting recesses into the bottom edge of the sides of the bookcase will make it easily manoeuvrable and gives the sides an elegant shape.

The feet
Ordinary wooden door knobs can be easily fitted to the underside of the bedside table instead of casters. They provide an attractive finishing touch.

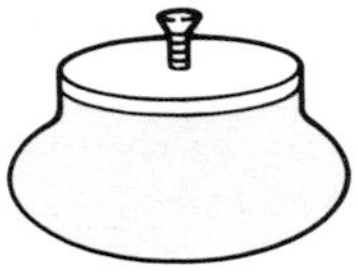

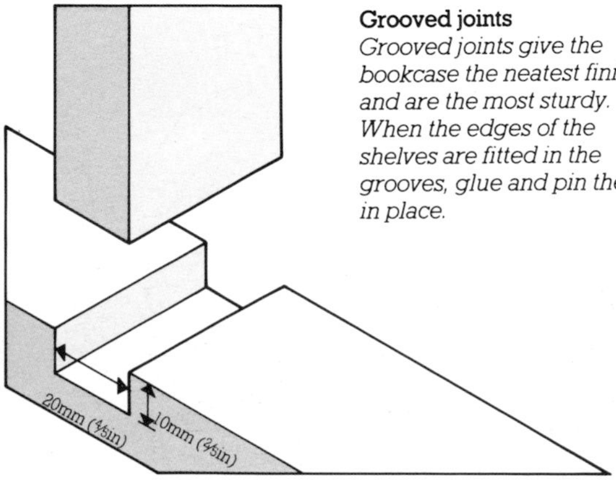
20mm (4/5in)
10mm (2/5in)

Grooved joints
Grooved joints give the bookcase the neatest finish and are the most sturdy. When the edges of the shelves are fitted in the grooves, glue and pin them in place.

MATERIALS AND EQUIPMENT			
Pieces			
1 Sides	2	810 x 240 x 20mm	(32 2/5 x 9 3/5 x 4/5in)
2 Long shelves	2	430 x 240 x 20mm	(17 1/5 x 9 3/5 x 4/5in)
3 Half shelf	1	215 x 240 x 20mm	(8 3/5 x 9 3/5 x 4/5in)
4 Divider	1	370 x 240 x 20mm	(14 4/5 x 9 3/5 x 4/5in)
Attachments			
Door knobs	4	Wooden (bedside table only)	
Equipment			
Saw, router or chisel, hammer, contact glue, panel pins, pencil for markings, ruler, set square, sandpaper, paintbrushes, primer and paint			

CHOCKS AWAY!

You can tell at a glance that my son Rupert is passionately fond of aeroplanes and cricket, so these were naturally the twin themes for me to use when decorating his room. Though it may not look like it, the 'blackboard' is actually painted on to the wall – I used green blackboard paint for this to create the feel of a 'cricket pitch – the numbers and lettering were added later to make a miniature scoreboard. I painted the batsmen and fielders freehand in eggshell, though you could use transfers, or a grid to create the design *(see pp60-1)*.

Apart from the bedside table and bed head, the furniture is dragged *(see p20)*. This, of course, is an attractive decorative technique in its own right, but here I also used it to create a nicely contrasting surface on which I could paint the aeroplane motifs I wanted to use as the unifying decorative theme. I carried this on to the bed head as well, painting it pastel blue and then creating a 'dog fight' straight from the days of *Those Magnificent Men In Their Flying Machines*.

Don't forget those little touches – like the mouse and mousehole at the base of the door. All of these will help you to make your scheme unique.

Stencil
Trace over this outline to get a simple motif you can use in your child's room.

Finding a framework
Make the most of existing features in a room, and turn them to your advantage. Here, I planned my design for this wall around the oak beams. Now they neatly frame the disparate elements of the blackboard, bed and chest of drawers.

Following curves
You will often achieve an attractive result by making a decoration follow the outlines of the piece of furniture on which you are working. The curve of this rainbow exactly matches that of the top of the bed head, and adds a sense of logic to the design.

Using appliqué
Remember that design doesn't have to be limited to walls and furniture. Even an appliqué in the simplest of patterns will add interest to a plain cushion.

Fitting a carpet
By the time your child starts school full-time, he or she will be old enough to have a carpet, if one has not already been fitted. Choose one that is durable without being too hard to sit on comfortably. It should also be in a neutral colour that doesn't show the dirt.

MAKING A BLACKBOARD

Blackboards are easy to make, even if you lack all experience at d-i-y. A simple blackboard takes very little time and effort to make. Blackboards can be made in any number of shapes and sizes, and will hang conveniently on a wall or door. Choose an interesting or amusing shape for your board – perhaps a favourite animal or cartoon character, a car, truck or train, an ice cream, a pineapple, or a jelly – but make sure you choose a shape with a relatively simple and distinctive outline, as it will appear in silhouette.

Choose a design from any source, and have it enlarged at a local photocopying shop *(see p128)*, or enlarge it yourself using a grid *(see pp60-1)*. Trace the design on 6-mm (¼-in) hardboard or plywood. Cut the shape out, and sand down the edges thoroughly. Paint the board with a coat of blackboard paint. Allow the paint to dry, and then apply the next coat. Allow this coat of paint to dry, and apply a third coat if you feel it is necessary.

When the blackboard paint is completely dry, add any extra finishing touches. Stencil *(see pp100-1)* the alphabet, or a few simple sums across the top; paint in some significant details, using enamel model paints *(see pp40-1)*. For example, if your blackboard is the shape of a house, paint in the outlines of the doors and windows; if your blackboard is the shape of a lorry, paint in the door of the driver's cab and the wheels.

Drill a hole in each of the two top corners of the blackboard, and thread them with strong picture cord. Knot the cord at the back. Hang the board at a height where it can be easily reached by your child.

Alternative blackboards

Blackboard paint can be painted straight on to walls, cupboards and even tables, so you can create a blackboard almost anywhere in the playroom, and build it into the decorative scheme of the room. Before painting any surface, make sure that it is as clean and smooth as possible, and wash or sand and repaint it if necessary. Paint an enormous blackboard on one wall, so that your children can indulge themselves with gigantic drawings and scribblings, or transform the doors of a cupboard.

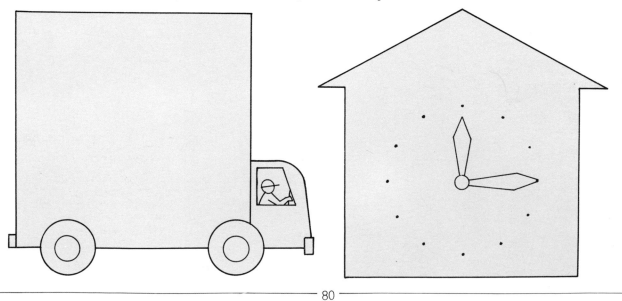

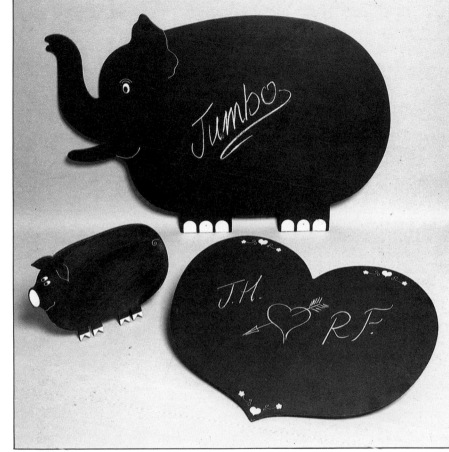

Black magic
A blackboard can be any shape or size. Choose a design that suits your child, and the character of the room. Here are a few suggestions to give you some inspiration.

Out of the ordinary
You can simply cut out the silhouette of an animal or toy, but painting details on to the blackboard with enamel paints (see pp40-1) can produce the most marvellous effects, and transforms an ordinary boat into a special Noah's Ark.

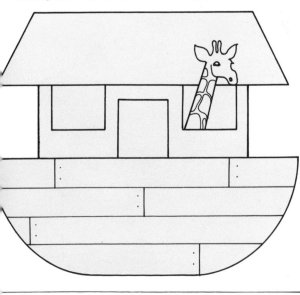

MATERIALS AND EQUIPMENT	
Pieces	
1 Board	appropriate length and width x 6mm (¼)
Attachments	
Hooks	Metal
Picture cord	
Equipment	
Saw, paintbrushes, ruler, pencil, sandpaper, compass (optional), drill, blackboard paint, paint for decoration (optional)	

A MOUSE'S 'AT HOME'

This, I think, shows you the ultimate in what murals can do in helping to create a total fantasy world in which children can lose themselves for hours. One half of the mural actually takes you into the mouse's hole, while the other section gives you a mouse-eye-view of the world outside.

Of course, creating an elaborate mural on this scale takes even a professional muralist days of planning and patient work. But the principles involved remain the same whatever the size or scope of subject *(see pp60-1)*. As well as determination, all that you basically need is an idea, however simple, that will transfer well to walls or ceilings. Remember that, in the majority of designs, one of the chief principles to observe is a proper sense of perspective, and that mistakes, though time-consuming, are not uncorrectable. You can always erase a mistake with paint solvent, or paint over it and try again!

A trick of the eye
Through the only object here which is 'real' is the fish tank, it looks to be part of the mural, which is inspired by Brambly Hedge.

Matching the mural
Careful planning of the objects in a room can really bring a mural to life. Here, the chair, pram, umbrella lampshade and the joke yellow teapot all match the mural in some way, and continue the theme of a lovely summer's day in the country. The pattern on the curtains – white birds flying on a blue background – blends in too.

Wooden washing line
This wooden batten has been pinned to the wall to give the impression of a washing line waving in the breeze above the eating mice. Metal coat hooks have been screwed into the wood at intervals, to take coats – and even a suit of armour! The right-hand side of the batten has been used to exhibit this child's paintings and drawings, which can be changed around at will.

Using wood
Skirting boards do not always have to be painted. These have been left in bare wood, and match the window seat. The motif of wood is continued with the curtain rail.

FABRIC PAINTING

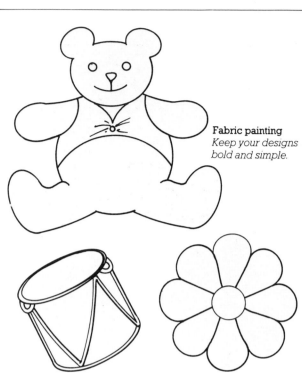

Fabric painting
Keep your designs bold and simple.

With the specially formulated paints that are now widely available, you can extend your own original interior design schemes to include fabrics. A painted motif on a chest of drawers can now be reflected in a curtain, lampshade or cushion cover, and, for instance, you can extend a painted design on a bedhead to include the bedspread as well.

Fabric paints are washable and durable. They come in a wide range of colours and are suitable for use on almost every type of material and no special preparations are necessary. All you have to do is iron your designs after the paint has thoroughly dried to seal them.

Choosing a design

Being able to paint directly on to fabric gives you enormous decorative scope, and you can achieve a marvellous variety of effects, from subtle and delicate shades to bold bright splashes of solid colour. If you are a confident artist, you can simply paint freehand on to your chosen fabric as though it were a canvas. Otherwise, you can trace or copy a design on to the fabric first before starting to paint. Having chosen a design, you can have it enlarged or reduced, if necessary, by a local photocopying shop. Alternatively, you can do this yourself using a grid (*see pp60-1*).

Tracing designs on to fabric

Tracing and transferring a design on to fabric can be difficult, since the surface is not smooth like wood, plastic or metal, and not firm enough always to guarantee a very clear or accurate outline. You will have to take great care if you plan to trace your design on to fabric, and avoid using intricate or finely detailed patterns.

Preparing to paint

You will need special fabric paint – no other paint will do – and different-sized art brushes. You will also need glass jars in which to mix your colours.

Before you begin work, ensure that the fabric you will be painting is as smooth and taut as possible. Folds and wrinkles in the material make painting much more difficult. You may find you have problems in achieving clear and even lines, and there is a greater risk of the paint smudging. If possible, use a tapestry frame in which to stretch the fabric while you are painting. Otherwise, before you begin work, iron the fabric to remove any wrinkles. Then place it on a flat surface, stretching it as tautly as possible and weighting it down at the edges.

Plan your overall design carefully before beginning work. You can sketch roughly and lightly on the fabric with tailors' chalk to get an idea of how your finished design will look. If you decide to trace and transfer a pattern, pin the tracings first to see what your design looks like. Always use tailors' chalk for sketching or drawing on fabric, not ball-point pen or even pencil, which may prove indelible. Remember, once you have begun to apply the paint to the fabric you will not be able to eradicate any mistakes as the paint immediately impregnates the cloth. It is therefore always prudent to begin with something modest and to practise first on some old material.

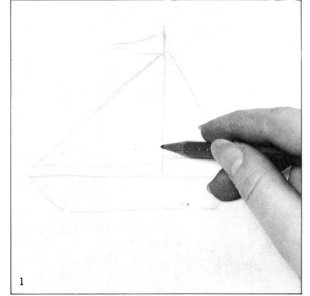

1

2

Allow the first colour to dry, and then apply the second. Allow that to dry, then apply the third and so on.

Do not attempt to correct errors with solvent, as you may only make matters worse. Instead try to blend any mistakes into the overall design, or camouflage them in some way.

3 When you have finished painting, and all the colours are completely dry, you must seal the paint. This is done by covering the fabric with a clean cotton cloth and pressing it with a hot iron.

Drawing or tracing a design

1 Draw or copy your chosen design directly on to the fabric with tailors' chalk, or, using a pencil, or fine felt-tip pen, trace the outline of your chosen design on to tracing paper. If you are tracing a design, use the following technique. Turn the tracing paper over and scribble over the outline with tailors' chalk. Never use pencil, which may mark the material permanently. Make sure you cover the line completely, but avoid scribbling over the entire tracing as this will increase the risk of smudging.

Put the tracing, with the original outline face upwards, on the fabric and pin it in place.

With a ball-point pen or pencil, trace over the original outline, pressing hard, so that the image is transferred to the fabric.

2 Paint in one colour at a time. Work in a logical progression – from left to right, or from top to bottom, for example – to minimize the risk of smudging the wet paint, and to ensure that you do not miss any areas to be painted.

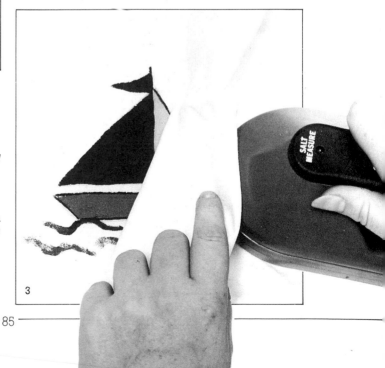

3

GROWING UP

They're changing guard at Buckingham
Palace -
Christopher Robin went down with Alice.
Alice is marrying one of the guard.
'A soldier's life is terrible hard,'
    Says Alice.

Buckingham Palace

A A Milne
1882-1956

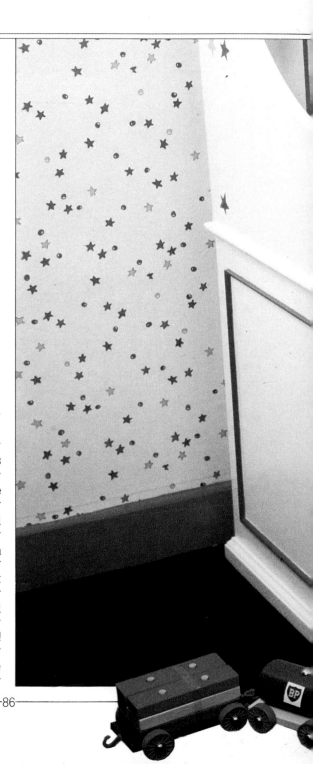

*Even a work area can be
made to look attractive,
given a little imagination.*

CONTENTS

WHAT EVERY PRE-TEENAGER NEEDS

By now, your child will be at school for most of the day, so the time he or she has at home will be more precious. Even if your child goes to boarding school, he or she will want an exciting bedroom at home. Whatever type of school your child attends, the bedroom will be very important, since it will be the room in which he or she can play and work. Try to make it as individual and interesting as possible.

Increasing the furniture

To encourage your child to do homework, you must provide somewhere in the room in which he or she can work. A desk with drawers is ideal, if there is enough space in the room. Buy an adjustable chair, so that your child can use it for the next few years, changing the height of the seat as necessary. If you make this work area attractive and interesting, it will be more conducive to hard work. Give your child a good source of artificial light by providing a brightly-coloured desk lamp that blends in with the colour scheme of the room, and pretty pencil holders.

Changing the floor-covering

Once your child reaches the age of eight, you should think of carpeting the room, if you have not already done so. There will be less likelihood of your child ruining a carpet through accidents now, and it will help to soundproof the room during your child's noisier moments. The room will also look warmer and cosier with a carpet.

The colour you choose must blend in with your existing design scheme, unless you think this is an ideal opportunity of redecorating the room. Do not be misled into believing that the darker the carpet, the less likely that any stains will show. As I know from bitter experience, a dark carpet will show up small specks of dirt and fluff, and you may have to spend a lot of time cleaning and vacuuming it. A white or cream carpet will be impractical for a child of this age, so you should choose one with a light pattern or that has two tones of colour.

Bunk beds

This is the perfect age for bunk beds. Your child will now be old enough to be able to sleep in a top bunk safely, without falling out. Bunks also save valuable floor space in a bedroom that is shared by two children.

Some bunk beds can be converted into two single beds, so that you can separate them later on. In the meantime, however, make them look as attractive as possible. If two of your children do share a room, and sleep in bunk beds, you could paint each child's name on his or her respective bed head, and paint the ladder in the same colour as the rest of the paintwork, or to tone in with the bedlinen. Matching duvet covers and pillowcases will make the beds look attractive, and also reduce the bother of bed-making. You could make your own duvet covers and pillowcases, by painting a design or motif on the fabric (see pp84-5).

Making a pinboard

Children love decorating their walls with posters, photographs of their favourite pop stars, animals, or anything else that appeals to them. Rather than making the room look bitty and disorganized by having pictures scattered all over the walls, you can make a pinboard and blackboard combined (see facing page), on which these can be fixed, and messages written.

Another way of doing this, and saving wall space, is to cover the door, or a cupboard, with cork tiles, thus leaving the walls free for other decorations, such as a mural. Your child will then be able to change the pictures as often as he or she likes. Remember that you do not have to leave the cork tiles completely bare when you have finished. You could paint your child's name on the top of the board, or stencil a design around the outside edges. Pay attention to the drawing pins, too, and buy some with heads painted in colours that match those in the room.

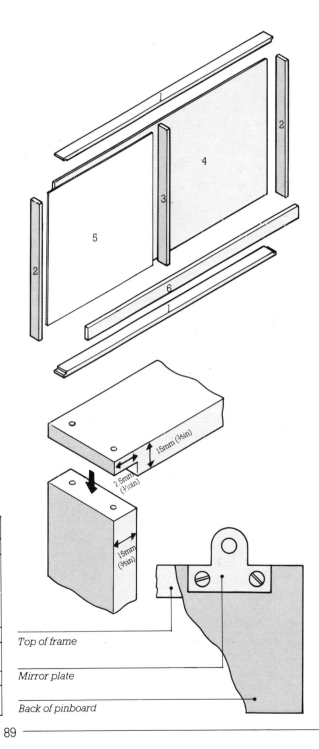

Making a pinboard/blackboard

The back (4) is made of hardboard, and the frame (1,2, 3, and 6) of pine.

Saw out all the pieces. Saw a groove, 15mm (⅗in) wide and 7.5mm (³⁄₁₀in) deep, at each end of the top and bottom (1). Countersink holes for the screws in the groove at each end of both pieces. Glue and screw the frame together.

Mark the centre points of the top and bottom pieces. Fix the centre divide (3) at

this point, using wood glue and panel pins.

Secure the hardboard back to the frame with panel pins. Cut the cork tiles to size and glue them in one half of the board. Paint the other half of the board with a coat of blackboard paint. Fix the shelf front (6) along the bottom front edge of the frame with panel pins.

Sand the edges of the pinboard smooth with sandpaper. Screw mirror plates in the top corners of the back of the board. Thread picture cord through the holes and knot it at the back.

15mm (⅗in)

7.5mm (³⁄₁₀in)

15mm (⅗in)

Top of frame

Mirror plate

Back of pinboard

MATERIALS AND EQUIPMENT			
Pieces			
1 Top and bottom	2	1000 x 40 x 15mm	(40 x 1⅗ x ⅗in)
2 Sides	2	485 x 40 x 15mm	(19⅖ x 1⅗ x ⅗in)
3 Divider	1	470 x 40 x15mm	(18⅘ x 1⅗ x ⅗in)
4 Back	1	1000 x 500mm	(40 x 20in)
5 Cork pinboard	1	470 x 477.5mm	(18⅘ x 19¹⁄₁₀in)
6 Shelf front	1	1000 x 40 x 15mm	(40 x 1⅗ x ⅗in)
Attachments			
Mirror plates	2	Metal	
Picture cord		2250mm (90in)	
Equipment			
Saw, hammer, screwdriver, drill, knife, screws, panel pins, sandpaper, wood glue, set square, pencil, ruler, blackboard paint			

SUGAR AND SPICE

As your children grow older, you will find that they take more and more interest in the decoration of their rooms. My policy is always to take such views into account, as otherwise the decoration will fail in the eyes of the child for whom it is intended. Tara, my younger daughter, played a major part in devising her room's decorative style. She started off by choosing the bedspread, from which I took the mice and flowers that are used as decorative motifs on the furniture and the door, while the squirrel family on the wall was also her idea. My job was to find a simple way of giving her what she wanted – something full of interest and charm – while preserving the original decorative style of the room as far as possible. To achieve this meant refining detail and mutually deciding on suitable decorative motifs.

From the photograph here, you might think the headboard of the bed is real – it is not. In fact, it is a *trompe l'oeil (see pp92-3)*, carefully created in paint to be as realistic as possible.

Using natural lines
Remember always to turn a feature into an advantage. The panels in this door gave me the idea of painting on a mouse standing on a swing.

Growing up
Children of this age group will have definite tastes, and you should allow them space to be able to express them fully.

Keep it fun!
One of the most engaging elements in any design is the humour behind it. Allow your wit, or that of your child, to shine through in small points of detail. For example, in this room, the mice skipping across the top of the trompe l'oeil bed head give an extra fillip to the scheme.

A line of squirrels
Always try to make your design fit the room. Although the original idea of the squirrels was Tara's, I had to ensure that they fitted into the room without appearing too obtrusive. Ranging them along the top of an oak beam was the ideal answer, as this gave them a natural focal point.

TROMPE L'OEIL

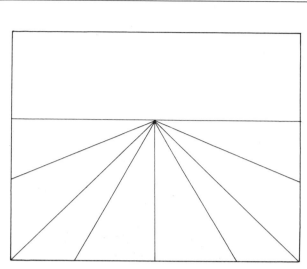

One of the most delightful and unusual ways of transforming your child's room is by creating a *trompe l'oeil*, which, literally translated, means to deceive the eye. Its possibilities are infinite, ranging from 'panelling' a plain flush door, to the evocation of a summer garden glimpsed through a french window.

Trompe l'oeil has the reputation of being extremely difficult, a technique that no amateur decorator should undertake lightly. This is a great pity, as many *trompe l'oeil* effects are within every enthusiast's reach.

Paint and paintbrushes

You can use acrylics, oils, or ordinary emulsion paint. You will need a wide range of colours, and a large selection of artists' brushes. When you have completed your *trompe l'oeil*, seal it with a coat of matt polyurethane varnish. This will protect and preserve it.

A smooth painting surface is vital as faults will distort your image, so sand and repaint any surface before beginning work.

Choosing a subject

Copy a painting, drawing or photograph, take a subject from a book or magazine *(see p128)*, or draw from life or your imagination. You can have any image enlarged or reduced at a local photocopying shop, or you can do it yourself using a grid *(see pp60-1)*.

Choosing a position

The positioning of a *trompe l'oeil* is all important. Use the natural features of the room as much as possible, and fill alcoves with false bookshelves, deceptive windows, and dolls' houses; paint mice escaping into imaginary holes in the skirting board or favourite animals peeping over the head of the bed; decorate mantelpieces or ledges with bunches of flowers, jars of sweets and toys. Aim for realism – an enormous vase on the mantel-

The horizon line
Irrespective of the size and dimensions of any object, its diagonal lines will always converge on the horizon line. Use this effect to give an impression of distance.

Drawing an ellipse
At an angle, a circle becomes an ellipse. To draw an ellipse, draw a circle inside a square and bisect it. Redraw the square at the required angle, bisect it, and then draw in the ellipse, which should touch the centre point of each side of the angled square.

piece, or a tiny clock face in the centre of a wall will look unnatural and ineffective.

Painting

Do practice sketches, and practise painting on painted board before you begin your *trompe l'oeil*. If you are painting a landscape, remember the importance of creating an impression of distance. When you are satisfied with your preliminary efforts, sketch in the outlines on your chosen surface with either pencil or charcoal. Paint as though you were painting on canvas, using every texture, tone, and colour.

Begin by painting in any large expanses of colour, and the background. Blend all the colours and tones carefully together. Add the fine details right at the end.

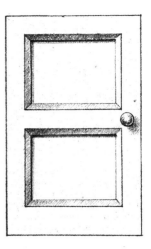

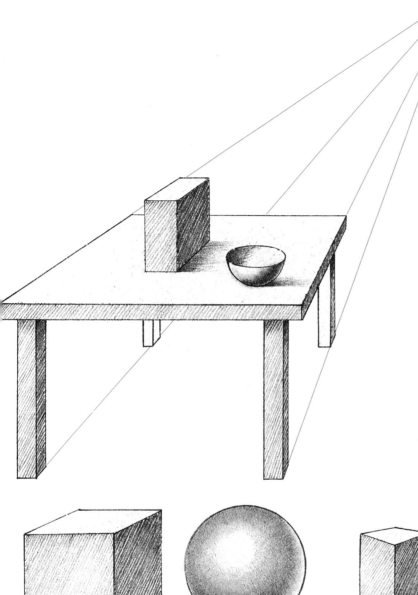

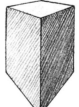

'Panelling' a door

Clean, sand and repaint the door. Use a flat or mid-sheen oil-based paint. Draw a line dividing the door horizontally, 130 to 180mm (5 to 7in) below the centre of the door. Draw the panel borders, 12mm (½in) wide, 100mm (3½in) in from the outside edge. Mitre the corners of the borders.

Mask the outside edges of the borders. This will guarantee a sharp outline. Mix a small amount of very thin medium-grey paint: mix 1 part white oil-based paint to 2 parts white spirit. Tint with raw umber, an artists' colourant.

Paint the bottom borders of each panel and the side borders furthest from the window. This gives the effect of a lighted panel edge. Paint up to the mitre lines. Darken the paint with a little more raw umber and paint the other borders to give the impression of a shadowed edge. When the paint is dry, peel off the masking tape.

Drag the door (see p20) with very pale grey paint, mixed as before. Brush the panels and sides of the door vertically, and the top, bottom, and centre of the door horizontally.

Allow to dry completely and coat with matt polyurethane varnish.

Dimension
Create an impression of three-dimensions by using shadows and highlights, graduating your colour with white or black. Remember, the closer an object is the clearer and more vivid it appears.

The effect of light
The angle from which light falls in a room, either from a window or artificial light, will determine the position of shadows and highlights. Use these shadows and highlights to give the illusion of shape and dimension.

Perspective
The laws of perspective are all important. If two planes of an object are visible, the parallel lines will appear to converge at a single vanishing point; if three planes are visible there will be two vanishing points.

PASTEL PERFECTION

Not every girl is fortunate enough to have a bedroom the size of Lucinda's, but equally there is little in this scheme that could not be adapted to suit a smaller space. The focal point is obviously the four-poster bed, with its pink hangings and frills. Having decided on these, which contrasted nicely with the room's existing panelling, the next logical step was to decorate Lucinda's dressing table in the same way to create an extremely feminine atmosphere.

If you decide to do something like this, a sense of colour – knowing which goes with what – is an extremely important element of your design. Here, having decided on the pastel pink, which appears in the fitted carpet and sweeping curtains, it was vital that the colour in which the furniture was painted did not fight against the atmosphere I was trying to create. The effect was heightened by dragging the paint *(see pp20-1)*. The delicate lines and rose motifs – all of which you can create for yourself – add that touch of class that I think can make any room unique.

Garlands
If you wish to decorate a room using the motif of a garland of flowers, you could trace this outline and use it to make a stencil.

Pretty storage
To accentuate the traditional feel of this room, I gave Lucinda a wooden chest in

which to store her clothes. I left the surface plain, but painted on elaborate garlands and floral patterns.

Instead of using flowers, you could make a motif out of an initial letter, and decorate that.

Draping furniture
By covering a dressing table and stool in a pretty material you can also hide a multitude of sins. This is the perfect way to decorate an old dressing table which is scratched but basically sound.

A PLACE TO WORK

As your children grow into adolescence, their needs and demands become those of adults, rather than children. They need the room to expand and develop their own interests and hobbies, to work, write letters or their diaries, play with their computers or their video games, draw, design, paint, just as they wish. This work station has been purpose-planned to accommodate all these activities, and also to provide a suitable home for a microcomputer, which is now becoming an integral part of every child's life.

Creating a specialized work and leisure area inside a child's own room is the perfect way of giving him or her room to grow up in. It incorporates a large work surface, shelves, and a pinboard, combining desk, bookshelves, bedside table and notice board all in one.

The work station provides plenty of space so that children can pursue all their favourite hobbies, using one half of the work surface for one project, and the other half for another. The shelves are within easy reach, and underneath the work station itself, there is plenty of room for storage.

The work station looks complex, but there is no need to be daunted by it. It is made of plywood and quite simple to build. You can make the work station a permanent construction by fixing it together with glue and screws, but if you fasten it with bolts, you can dismantle and reassemble it if the need arises.

Making the frames

The basis for the work station is the four frames (see diagram), one for each side. These are first built separately, and then bolted together at the corners to make the outside of the work station. Supports are then added for the floor, the shelves and work surfaces, and then the floor, shelves and surfaces themself just slip into place.

Mark the position of the joints on the horizontal rails of each of the four frames (4, 5, 7, 9, 10 and 12) as shown overleaf. Drill holes for the bolts through the rails at these points. Bolt the rails of each of the four frames in position (see over) to their respective uprights as follows: front frame, (2 and 3) to (4 and 5); back frame, (6) to (7); entrance end, (8) to (9 and 10); shelf end, (11) to (12). Make sure that all the joints are square, using a set square.

Bringing the frame together

There are two ways of fixing the four frames of the work station together – use either standard right-angled brackets, or specially prepared wooden blocks (see over).

Fix the four frames together at each corner, screwing either brackets or blocks down each of the corner uprights of the frames. Make sure that all the joints are square.

Fitting the floor support

With a pencil, mark the centre point on the bottom rails of the front and back rail. Fix the floor support rail (13) across the floor space, screwing it with either brackets or blocks to the rails of the front and back frames. Check that it is squarely set, and that the ends are flush with the sides of the rails. This floor support will give the floor extra strength.

Fit the floor (1), which should slip easily into place, on the support of the four frames and the floor support. If it does not fit easily at first, sand the edges a little. Fix the floor in place, using wood glue and panel pins.

Fitting the shelves and work surface

Fix the worktop support rail (14), which runs across the shelved end of the structure with brackets or blocks to the front and back frames. Check that the joints are square. Then fix the other worktop support rail (15), with brackets or blocks, again making sure that all the joints are square (see over). Lay the two parts of the worktop surface (16 and 17) on the worktop supports. Fix the worktop in place, using woodglue and panel pins.

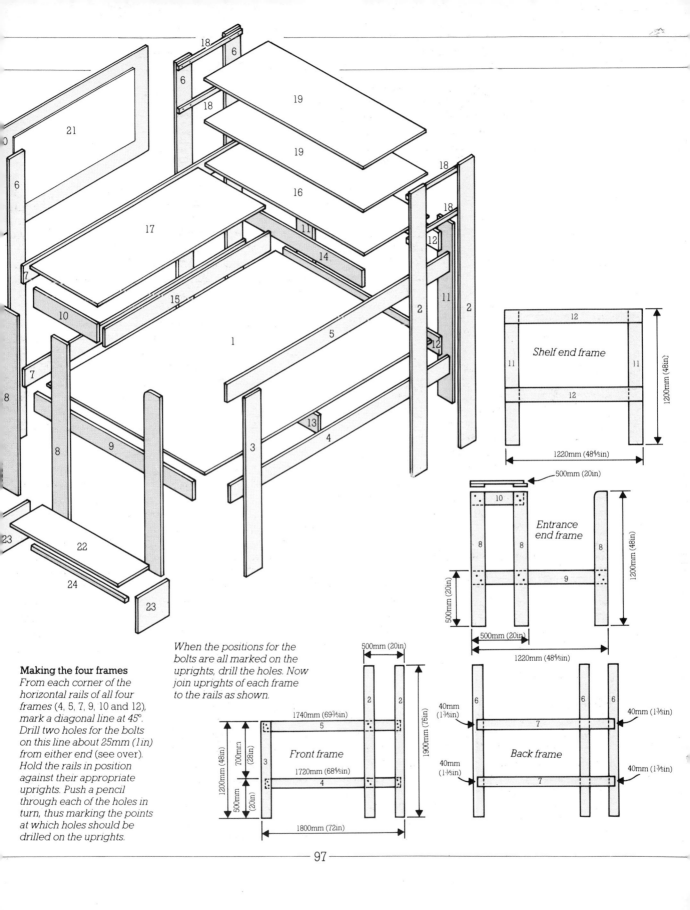

Making the four frames
From each corner of the horizontal rails of all four frames (4, 5, 7, 9, 10 and 12), mark a diagonal line at 45°. Drill two holes for the bolts on this line about 25mm (1in) from either end (see over). Hold the rails in position against their appropriate uprights. Push a pencil through each of the holes in turn, thus marking the points at which holes should be drilled on the uprights.

When the positions for the bolts are all marked on the uprights, drill the holes. Now join uprights of each frame to the rails as shown.

Shelf end frame

Entrance end frame

Front frame

Back frame

What a growing child needs
The most important thing you can give a growing child is room to develop. When your offspring become too old for playing with toys, and are no longer content to spend hours just running around in the garden, they need somewhere they can pursue more sophisticated and adult interests. You may not be able to provide them with their own private studies, but you can give them this marvellous study area that gives them plenty of room within an existing bedroom to do exactly as they please. It can be adapted to suit every individual child's needs and interests, and can cater for any number of different hobbies or interests. And it is a great help in keeping your children's bedrooms tidy, keeping all their mess well out of the way.

Measure the height of the shelves *(19)* according to your requirements. Mark the position of the shelves on the shelf uprights of the front and back frames *(2 and 6)*. Fix the shelf support battens *(18)* in position across the uprights, using panel pins, checking that they are squarely fixed. Fix the shelves to the battens with glue and panel pins.

Making the pinboard
Fix the backing for the pinboard *(20)* to the back of the uprights *(6)* of the back frame. Make sure that the top and sides of the board are flush with the top and sides of the uprights. Glue the actual pinboard *(21)* in between the uprights to the backing board.

Making the step
This is made of 18mm (¾in) chipboard. Cut all the pieces to size. With a pencil and ruler, mark

the centre point on each of the sides *(23)* – this is where the support *(24)* meets each side. With a drill and countersink bit, countersink holes for the screws at these points. Screw and glue the support rail in place. Check that it is squarely set.

Measure 180mm (7⅛in) in from the short sides of the top of the step *(22)*. Countersink two holes for screws on this line. Fix the top of the step to the sides with glue and screws.

The finishing touches
Sand the whole structure smooth and paint it as you wish. Leave it to your children to add the finishing touches. It is their work area, so let them fill the shelves and pin their own favourite pictures to the pinboard. However, providing a bright collection of stationery, and perhaps even some office equipment, such as a few filing trays, pencil holders and letter racks, may be a good idea.

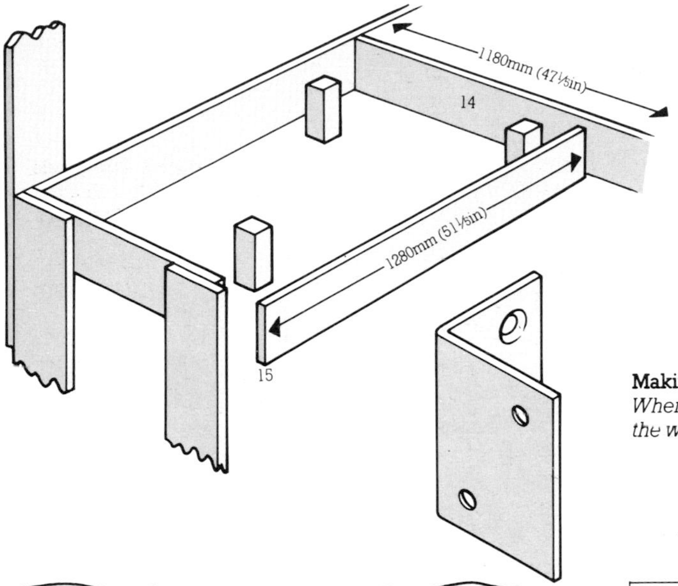

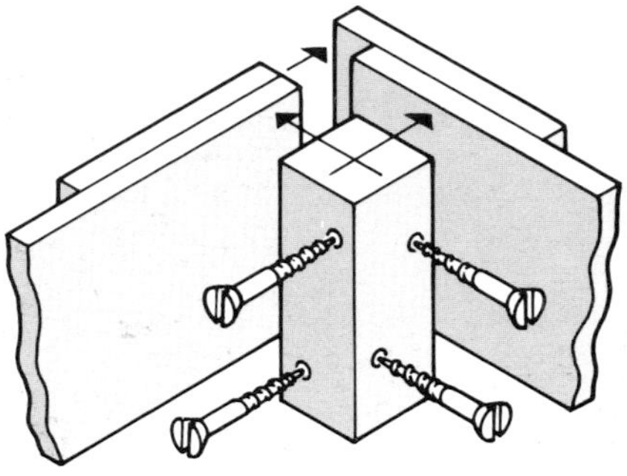

Making the work surface
When you fit the supports for the work surface, fasten them with blocks and screws or right-angled brackets for added strength.

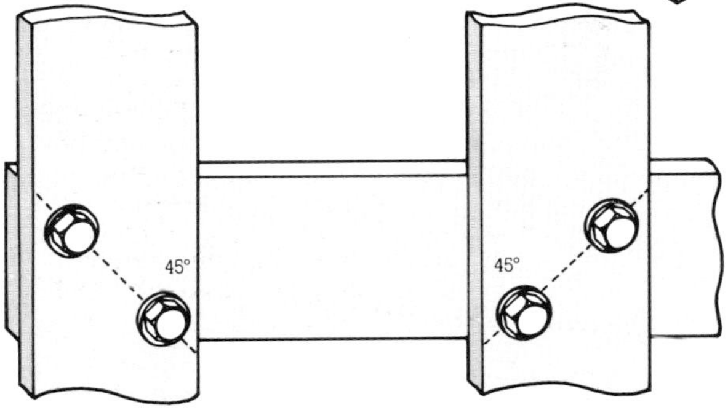

Joining the rails and uprights for the frames
If you are using bolts to fix the frames together, you must drill preliminary holes of the appropriate size in both the rails and the uprights of each frame, positioning them on each joint at an angle of 45° as shown here. For extra strength, the diagonal lines should run opposite to each other.

Secure the joints by pushing the bolts through and fastening them at the back with a washer and a nut as tightly as possible.

Screws and glue can be used instead of bolts.

Joining the frames and supports
Use specially-prepared wooden blocks for joining the frames and supports together or standard metal right-angled brackets.

To prepare wooden blocks, drill two holes in one side of the block, then two more in the side at right-angles to the first, as shown. Drill the second holes so that when the screws are inserted, they do not obstruct each other. The blocks join the frames together at each corner as shown. Check the corners are square, and screw the joints together.

MATERIALS AND EQUIPMENT

Pieces			
1 Floor	1	1220 x 1760 x 18mm	(48⅘ x 70⅖ x ¾in)
Front frame			
2 Shelf uprights	2	1900 x 120 x 20mm	(76 x 4⅘ x ⅘in)
3 End upright	1	1200 x 120 x 20mm	(48 x 4⅘ x ⅘in)
4 Lower rail	1	1720 x 120 x 20mm	(68⅘ x 4⅘ x ⅘in)
5 Upper rail	1	1740 x 120 x 20mm	(69⅗ x 4⅘ x ⅘in)
Back frame			
6 Uprights	2	1900 x 120 x 20mm	(76 x 4⅘ x ⅘in)
7 Rails	2	1720 x 120 x 20mm	(68⅘ x 4⅘ x ⅘in)
Entrance end frame			
8 Uprights	2	1200 x 120 x 20mm	(48 x 4⅘ x ⅘in)
9 Rail	1	1220 x 120 x 20mm	(48⅘ x 4⅕ x ⅘in)
10 Rail	1	480 x 120 x 20mm	(19⅕ x 4⅘ x ⅘in)
Shelf end frame			
11 Uprights	2	1200 x 120 x 20mm	(48 x 4⅘ x ⅘in)
12 Rails	2	1220 x 120 x 20mm	(48⅘ x 4⅘ x ⅘in)
13 Floor support	1	1180 x 120 x 20mm	(47⅕ x 4⅘ x ⅘)
14 Work top support	1	1180 x 120 x 20mm	(47⅕) x 4⅘ x ⅘in)
15 Work top support	1	1280 x 120 x 20mm	(51⅕ x 4⅘ x ⅘in)
16 Work top	1	1220 x 500 x 18mm	(48⅘ x 20 x ¾in)
17 Work top	1	1300 x 500 x 18mm	(52 x 20 x ¾in)
18 Shelf supports	4	500 x 30 x 30mm	(20 x 1⅕ x 1⅕in)
19 Shelves	3	1220 x 500 x 18mm	(48⅘ x 20 x 7/10in)
20 Pinboard backing	1	1420 x 700 x 6mm	(56⅘ x 28 x ¼in)
21 Pinboard	1	1280 x 700 x 20mm(max)	(51⅕ x 28 x ⅘in)
22 Step top	1	730 x 240 x 18mm	(29⅕ x 9⅗ x ¾in)
23 Step sides	2	270 x 240 x 18mm	(10⅘ x 9⅗ x ¾in)
24 Step support	1	334 x 40 x 20mm	(13⅖ x 1⅗ x ⅘in)
Attachments			
Blocks	16	Wooden	
or Brackets	16	Right-angled metal	

Equipment

Saw, hammer, screwdriver, drill, screws, panel pins, wood glue, bolts, drill, pencil, ruler, set square, sandpaper, paint

HOW TO STENCIL

This is the ideal technique for decorating larger surfaces, as it enables you to repeat a particular pattern or design an infinite number of times. It can be used on walls, on furniture and even floors. Stencilling a border along the top of wall can be an especially effective way of brightening up otherwise plain and ordinary paintwork.

Although stencilling may seem easier initially than tracing and transferring a design *(see pp40-1)*, great care is needed if the end result is going to look effective and professional. It is surprisingly easy to smudge edges, achieve an uneven texture, or not match the pattern properly, and so waste all your efforts. For this reason, practise the technique before you try to decorate either walls or furniture.

Choosing stencils

You can buy ready-made stencils from most good art shops, but with special stencil paper or an acetate sheet you can make your own. Stencil designs can be bought, which you can have enlarged (they are usually rather small) to the size you want at your local photocopying shop, or enlarge them yourself using a grid *(see pp60-1)*. However, you may prefer to trace a design for a stencil from a book, comic, wallpaper or fabric *(see p128)*, or to create your very own.

Preparing the surface

Any surface you intend to work on should first be washed or repainted if necessary. Use matt paint, either emulsion or oil-based. Then, you should plan carefully exactly where to position your stencilled design.

If you are stencilling in vertical or horizontal lines across a wall, you should draw in a guideline first in pencil. Check that your lines are strictly horizontal or vertical, using either a spirit level or a plumb line, and measure the distances between any parallel lines to make sure they are accurate. The same principal applies if you are painting a symmetrical design on a wall or a piece of furniture. You must mark exactly where the stencils must go before you begin – otherwise the end result will be uneven.

Paints and paintbrushes

You will need a special stencil brush. This resembles a shaving brush, and is available from most art shops. You also need a palate or dabbing board – however basic – as you should never dip a stencil brush directly into paint, because you will eventually ruin the fine texture of the bristles. Transfer the paint first on to the board, a little at a time. You can use any paint for stencilling. Emulsion paint is probably best, as you can easily correct mistakes by washing them off.

Mix enough of each colour you require in a tin, or jam jar, before beginning work – if you have to remix a colour, you may find it difficult to match the original shade. Remember that it is always better to mix too much paint than too little.

Stencilling
Stencilling is not always easy, but the effect it creates is marvellous. Its soft muted colours and warm texture is quite unique.

Cutting stencils

Trace your chosen design on to a piece of tracing paper, using a sharp pencil, or felt tip pen. Turn the tracing over, and scribble over the outline with a soft pencil, making sure it is completely covered.

Stick the tracing with masking tape on to the stencil board, leaving plenty of room between your outline and the edge of the stencil board. If you are using a multicoloured design you should transfer the complete design on to the appropriate number of stencil boards. For example, if you are using a three-coloured pattern, you will need three stencils, with the complete design traced on all three of them.

You need a firm wooden board or an old table to work on, as the surface will be scored when you cut the

stencils out. Use a scalpel or a very sharp knife. Cut out a different one-colour area on each stencil, so that one stencil has only the blue areas cut out, another one the red areas, and so on.

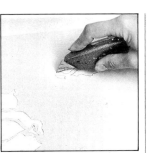

Make sure that you cut enough stencils to form the complete pattern.

Before you begin working or painting with your stencils, prepare your boards. Although it is easy to judge your stencilling accurately if your stencil boards are made of acetate, which is transparent, if your boards are made of card, you will have more difficulty. To prepare the stencils, put all the stencil boards together

with all the edges square, and then trim down the edges of each stencil board until they are all exactly the same size. Using a hole puncher, punch right through all the boards at the edges of the boards on each side. These holes will provide reference marks to help you align the stencils as you work.

Painting the stencil

Place the stencil in position on the wall, or piece of furniture, and secure it with masking tape. Mark its position with a pencil through the holes on each side. Use these marks to align subsequent stencils.

Transfer some paint on to your palate or board with an ordinary paint brush. Dip the stencil brush vertically into the paint on the board. Do not overfill the brush as you may blur the edges of the stencil as you paint, and spoil the delicate effect of stencilling. If you think the brush has too much paint on

it, dab it on to a piece of paper, to remove the excess. Holding the brush as upright as possible, paint through the holes in the stencil with a gentle dabbing motion. Do not apply the paint thickly, or

use too much pressure, as this will smudge the edges of the design.

When you have painted over the entire stencil, remove it, taking great care not to smudge the outlines. Wipe the stencil board clean, and check that there is no paint that will smudge on the wall.

Reposition it, carefully aligning it with the first stencil, by matching up the punched holes with the pencil reference marks on the wall if you are using a repeating pattern.

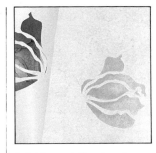

Paint through the stencil as before. Continue in this way until you have covered the required area. Allow the paint to dry thoroughly.

If your design involves more than one colour, take the next stencil, and position it where appropriate, using the marker dots made through your first stencil as a guide. If you are using acetate sheet, you should be able to see where the stencil should go. Continue until you have stencilled all the second colour areas, and allow the paint to dry. Stencil the third colour areas, and so on.

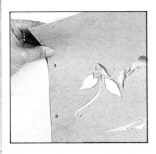

When you have completed the entire design, it is a good idea to varnish the surface with a clear matt polyurethane varnish. This will help protect and preserve the design.

If you are using emulsion and make a mistake, simply wash it off. If you are using an oil-based paint, wipe it off with a rag or tissue soaked in a little turpentine or white spirit. If you make a very bad mistake, you can paint over it when the paint is dry.

GREEN FOR GO!

Individuality need not be costly. Here is a teenage room full of style and character, simply and inexpensively created through the use of paint and a little imagination.

The bold, striking choice of green for the walls gives this room a clean, bright look; the real trick, however, is in the extension of the colour over the picture rail to create the carefully-devised minarets on the border area between walls and ceiling. Of course, you could use other devices and patterns – the choice depends on individual taste and the dimensions of the room you are planning to decorate.

By keeping things simple, you will not only cut down the work involved. You will also create a stimulating basis that your teenager can develop to give the room a personal touch, as the collage here shows. If this idea appeals to both of you, take care to choose a suitable background colour for the walls so that the collage is not over-powered.

Bare wood
If your window frames are in good condition, and the wood is attractive, you could leave them unpainted. Just cover them with a coat of wood stainer, and then varnish, if you want a shiny finish. This gives an unusual finish to a room, and provides an interesting contrast between the bare wood and the painted or papered walls.

Keep it plain
With a dramatic wall design such as this, you should keep the rest of the room simple, so as not to detract from it. The plain white storage units in this room are a perfect decorative foil for the borders.

Using borders
A border of colours can make all the difference to a room, and lead the eye to an area you wish to emphasize. Remember that it does not always have to be at the top of a wall – you could paint a border, such as one of designs shown here, along a skirting board, or halfway up a wall.

Finding inspiration
You will be able to achieve exciting effects if you allow your basic design scheme to inspire the furniture decoration. In this room, the minarets created by the border are echoed in the oriental feel of the small wooden chair and the rich-looking rug.

APPLIQUÉ

Bolder, brighter and warmer than either embroidery or fabric paint, appliqué is perfect for use in your child's room and can transform a plain or drab bedspread, or a pile of ordinary cushions, into the focal point of a room. There is no need for elaborate designs – stick to simple designs and concentrate on dramatic colours and fabric textures, which, by themselves, create the most delightful effects.

You can use almost any material for appliqué, and so have a vast range of colours, patterns and textures at your disposal. Use up leftover scraps from dressmaking, old clothes, or buy patchwork scraps available from many fabric shops. However, you must use compatible fabrics. Avoid using nylon on linen for example, as they have to be cleaned in completely different ways, and dark, non-fast coloured materials on pale backgrounds. By following these few basic rules you should be able to wash or clean any article without difficulty.

Choosing a design

You may wish to develop or extend a motif or design you are creating in paper or paint elsewhere in the room, or simply wish to add a splash of colour to an otherwise dull expanse of fabric. Whichever is the case, when choosing a design, you should bear in mind that working with small pieces of material can be difficult and fiddly. It is almost inevitable that the fabric will become slightly distorted while you are working, and the material may even begin to fray. As a result, you will have to take particular care with small pieces of material and delicate designs to minimize these effects. Always handle the appliqué pieces gently, and avoid fiddling with them unnecessarily. If you think there is a risk of any material fraying badly, you can sew a running stitch around the outside of each piece. Plan the overall design of your appliqué first, and decide which colours and fabrics you are going to use.

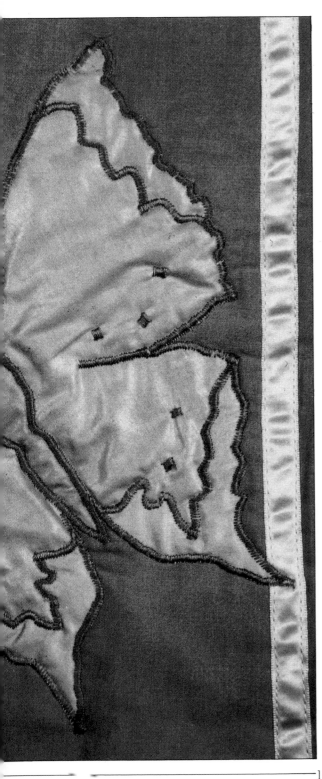

Sewing an appliqué

Have your design enlarged or reduced to an appropriate size. Choose a design that can be clearly divided into parts, so that it can easily be translated into a pattern.

Draw, or trace your chosen design on to dressmakers' pattern paper and cut it out.

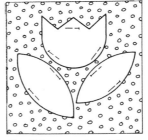

Pin all the paper templates on to your base fabric, and make sure that the design works in practice. Adjust your pattern if necessary.

When you are completely satisfied, mark on the base fabric where each part of the design is to be positioned, using tailors' chalk.

Pin each template to the appropriate fabric, and cut out each shape, leaving an extra 3mm (¹/₈in) all round to allow for stitching.

Cut out each shape again in the same way from medium weight non-woven interfacing. This will act as a backing for the appliqué. If you want to give the appliqué a thicker, richer texture, you can cut out a third slightly smaller shape from Terylene wadding. This should be placed between the fabric and the interfacing.

Pin each piece of fabric to its backing, incorporating the wadding if it is being used, and then pin both in place on your base fabric.

Tack each shape in place. Make sure there are no folds or wrinkles in either the shape or the material beneath.

Use a sewing machine to satin stitch around all the raw edges of each shape. Check that they all lie smoothly together. You can also do this by hand, but it will take some time.

When you have stitched all the pieces together, press the finished article with a warm iron.

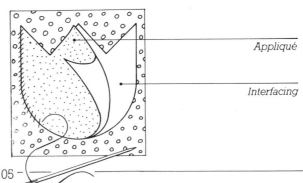

Appliqué

Interfacing

INTO THE TEENS

I'm sorry you are wiser,
I'm sorry you are taller;
I liked you better foolish
And I liked you better smaller!

For Teenagers

Anon

By the time your child becomes a teenager, he or she will want a room that expresses his or her personality.

CONTENTS

WHAT EVERY TEENAGER NEEDS

It is a very important occasion when your child becomes a teenager. He or she will feel that the days of childhood are over, and will want a bedroom that is adult, and reflects his or her new status and interests. The older your teenager becomes, the more the room should be seen as an extension of his or her personality, so it is important that its decoration is discussed between the two of you.

Teenagers enjoy entertaining their friends in their bedrooms, sitting on the floor and on chairs, listening to music, talking and drinking coffee. You should therefore cater for these needs when you plan the room.

Living with loud music

For most teenagers, their first hi-fi unit will hold pride of place. They will spend hours sitting in their room, working, or relaxing, and listening to music. To save unnecessary arguments about noise, try to fit thick carpets and curtains which will help to soundproof the room by deadening some of the noise. Removing the doors from wardrobes, and replacing them with a curtain that blends in with the rest of the room, will also help to absorb the sound. Make a simple unit in which your teenager can store the records and tapes when they are not in use *(see facing page)*.

Creating a work area

The most important consideration in a room for someone of this age group is that it should be a place in which the teenager can work. He or she will spend a lot of time studying for important exams, and this is hard enough anyway, without expecting the teenager to work in cramped or crowded surroundings.

Ideally, you should put a desk, with a good source of light, nearby bookshelves, and a comfortable chair, in the bedroom. You can build your own work desk, which can also accommodate a computer *(see pp96-9)*.

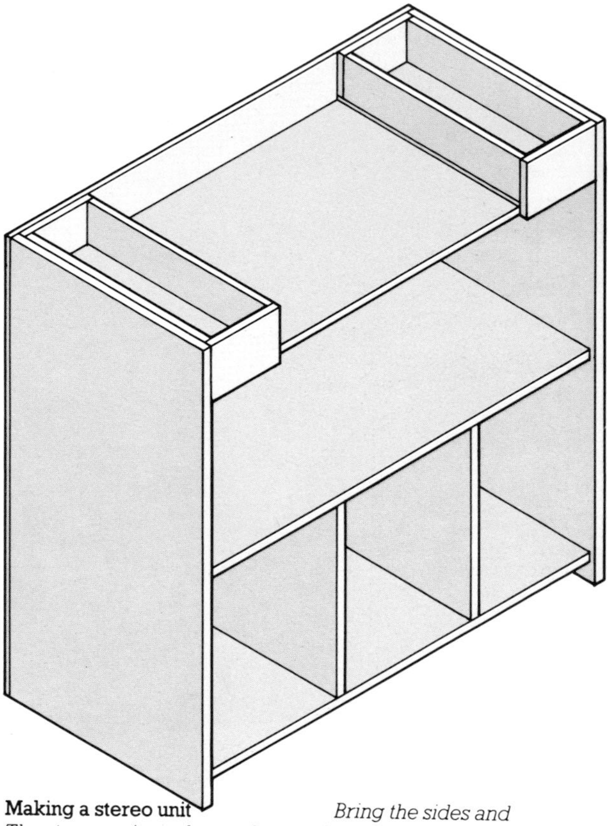

Making a stereo unit

The stereo unit can be made of ordinary plywood or the melamine-faced variety. Mark out all the pieces with a ruler and pencil and cut them with a saw.

Mark out the positions for the screws on both sides (2) as shown. Drill a hole at each point, and then countersink each hole using a countersink bit.

Bring the sides and shelves (1) together, and fix the shelves to the sides lightly with panel pins – this will keep the shelves in position while you secure them permanently with the screws. Check that all the joints are square with a set square and then fix the shelves firmly to the sides using wood glue and screws.

MATERIALS AND EQUIPMENT

Pieces			
1 Shelves	3	800 x 380 x 15mm	(32 x 15⅕ x ⅗in)
2 Sides	2	820 x 400 x 15mm	(32⅘ x 16 x ⅗in)
3 Back	1	830 x 820 x 15mm	(33⅕ x 32⅘ x ⅗in)
4 Shelf dividers	2	380 x 345 x 15mm	(15⅕ x 13⅘ x ⅗in)
5 Box sides	4	368 x 65 x 12mm	(14¾ x 2⅗ x ½in)
6 Box front ends	2	94 x 140 x 12mm	(3¾ x 5⅗ x ½in)
7 Box back ends	2	65 x 140 x 12mm	(2⅗ x 5⅗ x ½in)
8 Box bottoms	2	380 x 140 x 12mm	(15⅕ x 5⅗ x ½in)

Equipment

Saw, drill, screwdriver, countersink bit, hammer, screws, panel pins, wood glue, ruler, pencil for marking, set square, paint or varnish

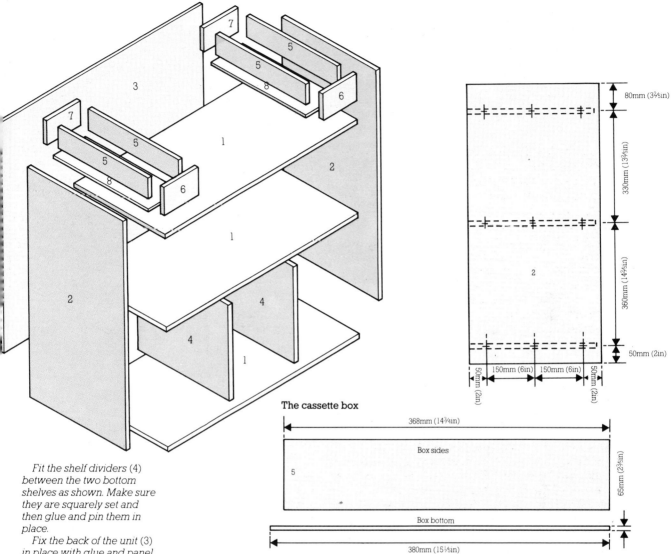

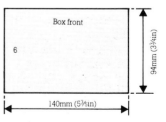

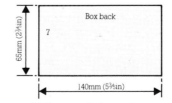

The cassette box

Box sides

Box bottom

368mm (14¾in)

380mm (15⅛in)

65mm (2⅗in)

5

Box back

7

Box front

6

65mm (2⅗in)

140mm (5⅗in)

94mm (3¾in)

140mm (5⅗in)

80mm (3⅖in)

330mm (13⅖in)

360mm (14⅖in)

50mm (2in)

50mm (2in)

150mm (6in)

150mm (6in)

50mm (2in)

2

Fit the shelf dividers (4) between the two bottom shelves as shown. Make sure they are squarely set and then glue and pin them in place.

Fix the back of the unit (3) in place with glue and panel pins. This will help to give the unit extra strength. When you have decided how to arrange your stereo equipment on the unit, drill holes in the back at the appropriate points to allow the wires of the equipment to pass through.

leaving the lower edge of the front end to overlap the bottom of the sides by 17mm (⁷⁄₁₀in). Glue and pin the bottoms (8) of the boxes in place.

Making the cassette boxes

Fix the sides of the cassette boxes (5) to the back ends (7) with glue and panel pins, making sure the corners are square. Fix the front ends in place (6) in the same way,

The finishing touches

Sand the unit and the boxes smooth, and paint them with primer. Allow this to dry and then add a top coat. Alternatively you can varnish the unit.

Fit the cassette boxes in place on top of the stereo unit, making sure they fit squarely on the shelf. Allow the boxes to sit freely on the shelves, so you can move them as you wish.

SOMETHING CHIC

If you are starting to decorate a room from scratch, remember that everything in it – this includes fabrics and furnishings, as well as paint and wallpaper – should work to contribute to the overall effect. This room, designed for a fairly sophisticated teenager, is a good example of the dividends a little forethought can produce. Like most teenagers, Tara, the girl for whom the room was designed, is fashion-conscious, so, when I planned the scheme, I bore this and her personal likes and dislikes very much in mind.

The alcove proved a problem, until I decided to put a four-poster bed into it. This is not as extravagant as it might appear. There is no need to buy a four-poster – you can simply screw supports into a conventional bed's framework, disguising them with hangings.

Faking a four-poster
Very often, it is possible to 'cheat' a feature. Here, for example, I would have blocked off light from the window if I had given the bed complete hangings. However, I solved the problem by just putting fake hangings at the top of the bed.

Simple and sophisticated
Do not be frightened of keeping a surface simple when you think it is necessary. This table lamp was left undecorated to provide a contrast with the rest of the room. The secret of good design is knowing when to leave well alone, as well as knowing when to decorate.

Border lines
The pervading motif of this room – a spray of flowers – was so delicate that it would have been lost on the chest if I had not painted border lines of pink and blue around the drawers, to box in the motif and give it a framework.

Creating an atmosphere
The four-poster bed gave a formal, sophisticated feel to this room, so the rest of the furniture had to complement it for the design to work. The skirt around the bottom of this chair exactly matched the rich ruffles of the curtains and bed hangings.

A dummy clock
Remember that objects in a room do not always have to be practical – sometimes they can be purely decorative. This sophisticated-looking clock doesn't actually work. Rather than tell the time, it echoes the design of the wallpaper, and bears the name of Tara, the girl whose room this is.

BORDERS AND TRIMS

A pretty border or trim is the perfect way to add a finishing flourish. Although you can buy borderings, creating your own original borders on walls fabric and furniture is well worth the time it takes.

There are variety of techniques you can use for creating a decorative border, depending on your material. There is an almost infinite variety of designs you can use for bordering. Only a few suggestions are given below, so experiment a little with different ideas. Even the simplest border will brighten up anything, but why not also be more ambitious? Stencilling *(see pp100-1)*, appliqué *(see pp104-5)*, painting on fabric *(see pp84-5)* and on furniture *(see pp40-1)* are all techniques you have at your command.

Painting on furniture
The surface you will be working on should be as smooth and clean as possible. The best paint to

Borders
A pretty border provides the perfect finishing touch. Use straight or curved lines, continuous or broken; use thick lines or thin, double or single; use dots, dashes and diagonals. Remember the charms of simple designs – a single line can often be quite as effective as the most elaborate flourish.

use for painting furniture is enamel model paint *(see pp40-1)*. However, if you are stencilling *(see pp100-1)* you should use emulsion paint, and then seal the design afterwards with a matt varnish.

You will need a variety of brushes – if you intend to stencil you will need a special stencilling brush. Otherwise a selection of art brushes of varying thicknesses will be adequate. You will also need tracing paper and glass jars for mixing paints *(see pp40-1)*.

Make sure that everything is ready before you begin to work. Always mix enough paint to cover all the required area, so that you can count on the same shade and tone throughout.

A comfortable working position
Painting a decorative border takes time and patience, so it is essential that you are comfortable while you are working. A steady hand is also vital. If you are painting a piece of furniture, keep the surface you are painting as horizontal as possible. Also, before you start, work out the easiest way of manoeuvring the article you are decorating while you are painting. If you are painting the wall, make sure you can easily reach the area on which you are working.

Measuring guidelines
Unless you are painting beading, which in itself acts as your guideline, you must carefully measure the line or lines your border will follow. Draw in your guidelines with a pencil. Make sure that all your lines are equidistant from the relevant edges, and that lines running parallel really are parallel.

Painting or stencilling a decorative border
Plan and measure your border carefully in advance, especially if you use a repeating pattern, in which regularity is all important. Roughly draw or trace in the entire design before you begin work. It is easier to correct mistakes at this stage than when you have begun painting. Having drawn in the guidelines, create your decorative border using your chosen technique.

Beading

Painting the beading on furniture and other woodwork is quite straightforward. Masking off either side of the beading for a clean edge, paint along the line of the beading. Correct any mistakes when the paint is dry with a paper tissue soaked in a little turpentine or white spirit.

Lining

Draw in your guidelines (above). If your hand is unsteady, mask the edges of the line with masking tape, which prevents paint running over the edges of the line. Remove the tape before the paint dries to soften any ridges.

If you do not use masking tape, paint first along the edges of the line, and then fill in the centre, with even brush strokes along the length of the line (below). When dry, correct mistakes with a little turpentine or white spirit. Do not try to straighten the edges of the line – you will probably only succeed in making them more uneven and blurred.

Broken lining

This is easy and effective. Having drawn in the guidelines, paint roughly along the length of the lines. Do not worry about any irregularities – they are an integral part of the charm of broken lining. You can either paint in a continuous line, or in a series of dashes of variable length.

TOP OF THE POPS

Geometric lines and brightly coloured wallpapers and fabrics provide a firm design basis for this ultra-modern room, with its cool, 'laid back' character. From ceiling to floor level, the contrasting patterns say it all – this is a living space for a contemporary teenager.

If you have the wall space, use it. A bedside wall is an ideal spot for a giant pinboard, for instance. Rather than filling the room with furniture, which would take up much of the space this scheme was designed to emphasize, you could make bean bags *(see pp68-9)* and use them as a method of seating instead. These are not only comfortable; they also provide that informal touch which most teenagers take considerable pains to cultivate.

There are other finishing touches you can consider adding as well. You could embroider a duvet cover, for instance, in a design that matches the wallpaper pattern, or hand paint the window blinds with a motif that appears elsewhere in the room.

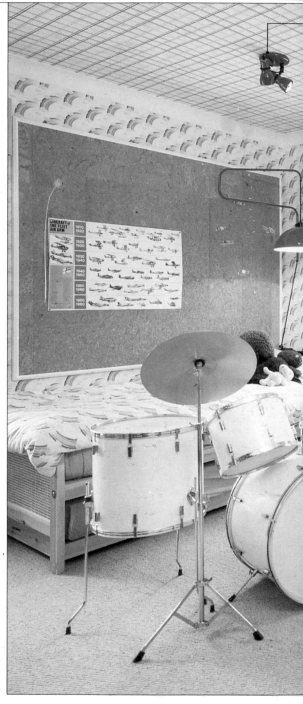

Bold colour
All the accessories are in just one colour in this room – a theme continued on to the wardrobe, which is painted in pillar box red.

Linked lighting
Instead of choosing one large central ceiling light, I used several lights in this room, and gave them all bright red shades, to match the colour of the bean bag and the red in the wallpapers.

Mix and match
Don't feel confined to using just one wallpaper in a room. Here, I chose two wallpaper designs, then planned the rest of my design around them. I then decided to link them, using their common primary colours of red, blue and yellow, and covered the curtains in stripes of those colours, which I sewed on with appliqué.

The best of both worlds
If you can't decide whether to fit blinds or curtains, why not have both. This is an especially effective device if you choose blinds in the same fabric as the wallpaper, or paint them with a trompe l'oeil scene.

Finding a work space
It is very important for teenagers to have somewhere in their rooms at which to work. Make sure the area is well lit to avoid eye-strain, and that the chair is the right height for the teenager to be able to work comfortably at the desk or table.

MAKING A WORKBENCH

The practical answer
For the young d-i-y

enthusiast, a solid and hard-wearing workbench is vital.

Children of every age are creative, and love making things with their hands and the more you encourage them the better so, as they grow out of the age of pipecleaners and plasticene, a traditional workbench is an essential asset. And helping you to make the workbench can be your child's first project.

The legs and rails of the table are made of pine, to provide the necessary strength; the shelf is plywood, and the top surface can either be chipboard or, if you want it to be more professional and hard-wearing, solid timber. Although the depth for the top surface is given here as 18mm (¾in), this only refers to plywood. If you use timber, it should be 25mm (1in) thick.

Making the frame

With a pencil and ruler, mark out the top and bottom rails (2, 3, 4, 5, 6 and 7) and the legs (9) of the workbench. Although a standard measurement of 700mm (28in) is given here for the length of the legs, you can make them longer or shorter, depending upon the height of your child. Remember that he or she must be able to work comfortably at the workbench.

Saw out all the pieces. Saw the corners off the bottom of the front and back top rails (2 and 3). This gives a smoother neater finish to the work top. Mark and saw out the half joints at the ends of the side bottom rails (7). These should be 20mm (⅘in) deep and 45mm (1⅘in) wide. Mark out the grooved joints on the front and back bottom rails (5 and 6). These should be positioned 75mm (3in) from the end of the rails, and should be 20mm (⅘in) deep and 70mm (2⅘in) wide. Cut out the grooves by sawing down the sides of the grooves, and then chiselling out the centre. Make sure that all the grooves are absolutely square and smooth, and fit easily around the legs of the workbench.

Saw out the work top (1) and the shelf (8). Cut a rectangular piece 45 x 70mm (1⅘ x 2⅘in)

from each of the corners of the shelf so it fits neatly around the legs.

Assembling the workbench

Sand all the parts of the workbench thoroughly before assembly. Countersink holes for the screws in the joints of the front and back bottom rails (5 and 6), using a drill and countersink bit. Fit the rails around the legs (9), 150mm (6in) from the bottom of the legs, and screw them in place. Countersink holes in the joints of the bottom side rails (7). Fit them over the front and back bottom rails, and screw them in place, making sure that that they are flush with the legs and with the front and back rails.

Countersink holes for the screws in the front (2), back (3) and side (4) top rails. Screw them to the top of the legs. Check that all the rails are flush with the legs.

Slip the shelf (8) into place, so that it rests on top of the bottom rails. Fix the shelf to the rails, using panel pins and wood glue. Countersink holes for the screws around the edge of the work top (1). Screw the table top in place.

The finishing touches

Fill all the screw holes with proprietary filler. When this is dry sand the whole workbench smooth.

Making a bench hook

A bench hook holds wood steady while you work. To make it, cut a 250-mm (10-in) square of 6-mm (1/4-in) plywood, glue a 250-mm (10-in) length of batten to one side and a 130-mm (51/5-in) length of batten to other side.

The lower batten grips the edge of the table, while you can hold any piece of wood you are cutting against the firm edge of the upper batten. This keeps the wood straight and in place, enabling you to work more easily.

Grooved joints
These provide a strong supportive frame for the workbench. Screw through the rail into the leg.

45mm (13/4in)
70mm (23/4in)
20mm (4/5in)
70mm (23/4in)
75mm (3in)

MATERIALS AND EQUIPMENT			
Pieces			
1 Top	1	1220 x 450 x 18mm	(481/5 x 18 x 3/4in)
2 Front top rail	1	1220 x 145 x 25mm	(481/5 x 55/5 x 1in)
3 Back top rail	1	1220 x 145 x 25mm	(481/5 x .51/5 x 1in)
4 Side rails	2	400 x 145 x 25mm	(16 x 55/5 x 1in)
5 Front bottom rail	1	1220 x 45 x 70mm	(481/5 x 11/5 x 23/5in)
6 Back bottom rail	1	1220 x 45 x 70mm	(481/5 x 11/5 x 23/5in)
7 Side bottom rails	2	400 x 45 x 70mm	(16 x 11/5 x 23/5in)
8 Shelf	1	1070 x 350 x 12mm	(421/5 x 14 x 1/2in)
9 Legs	4	700 x 70 x 45mm	(28 x 23/5 x 11/5in)
Equipment			
Saw, hammer, screwdriver, chisel, drill, wood glue, panel pins, screws, pencil for marking, ruler, set square, sandpaper			

SIMPLE SOPHISTICATION

Though it may sound contradictory, there is no reason for sophistication not to be simple. As children grow into their teens, what I generally aim to do is to provide the basics of a decorative scheme, on which they themselves can build. This way, I hope, they will be encouraged to develop ideas that reflect their own tastes and interests.

In this room, I wanted to maintain the naturally light and airy look; and keeping things simple was an obvious aim. I find one of best ways of achieving this is to start from the fabrics, but, if you take this route, remember that their cost will be your greatest expense by far. Choose them carefully and plan the rest of the decoration around them, picking up suitable motifs and carrying them through the room. You can see, for instance, that the motifs from the fabrics used for the bedspread and curtains have been carried on to the dressing table.

Sloping walls
Decorating the walls of an irregularly-shaped room can pose problems. Here, I decided to treat the variously-angled walls as one surface, and paint them in a single unifying colour.

Effective edging
Sometimes a simple border on a curtain can make all the difference to a room, giving it an added impact. The pink border at the top and bottom of this pelmet naturally leads the eye to the pink walls, and accentuates the pink in the curtain material. Note that the valance around the bed has been given a similar edging device.

Concealing a radiator
Radiators are not always positioned exactly where you would like! If this is the case, paint them to blend in with the rest of your colour scheme. In this room, I painted the radiator in the same colour as the walls to make it less obtrusive.

Giving definition
The fabric motif was used to decorate the dressing table, which was given its own character and definition by the addition of formal blue border lines around the drawers and cupboards.

Mixing fabric designs
Be bold in your use of fabrics. Sometimes two contrasting designs work very well together, and each will lend an extra dimension to the other. Here, the frill around the duvet cover accentuates the ruff around the bottom of the valance, although the patterns of the materials are quite different.

A DRESSING TABLE

Every teenage girl should have her own dressing table in which to keep her newly-acquired collections of make-up, jewellery, hair slides and other small oddments. The dressing table shown here is made of birch plywood with pine rails and panels, and is both simple and elegant.

Making the frame

Saw out all the pieces for the dressing table. Mark the position for the moulding *(7 and 8)* on the front panel *(5)*, as shown in the main diagram.

Using a jig saw, cut decorative heart-shaped holes in the centre of each side panel *(1)*, if you wish, and cut out a shallow curve at the bottom of each panel.

Fix the support battens *(9)* along the bottom edge of the two panels *(5)*, using wood glue and panel pins. Make sure that each batten is square with the edge of the panel, as they will provide the support for the base of the dressing table.

To position the panels, mark the holes for the screws in the side panels *(1)*, as shown in the diagram. This diagram shows only the outside surface of the left-hand side panel – on the outside surface of the right-hand panel, all the markings will be positioned on the opposite side to those shown here. Countersink holes at these points, using a drill and a countersink bit. Fix the front and back panels *(5)* and the rail *(10)* in place, using wood glue and screws. Make sure that the ends of the front and back panels and the rail are flush with the side panels. Also check that the joints are all square, using a set square. Fill all the countersink holes with proprietary filler.

The compartments and the lids

Fit the base *(2)* of the dressing table into the frame and fix it to the support battens with wood glue and panel pins. Check that the edges of the base are flush with the front and back panels and sides. With a pencil and ruler, mark the centre of both the front and back panels. Insert the centre

The professional finish
The dressing table is a marvellous piece of bedroom furniture. Leave it a plain white, or paint it with your own designs (see pp40-1).

divider *(4)* at this point. Make sure that it fits squarely, using a set square. Fix the divider to the front and back panels and the base with glue and panel pins.

Pin the lid moulding *(6)* along the front edge of the lids *(3)*. Fix the mirror, as shown, inside one of the lids, using glue or proprietary metal screw corners. Attach the lids to the back panel of the dressing table with a continuous piano hinge. Make sure the hinge is squarely set or the lids will not close properly. Screw in four eyes – one 200mm (8in) from the bottom on the inside edge of each lid of the dressing table, and one to each side of the centre divider, 200mm (8in) from the back of the dressing table. Fasten a 325-mm (13-in) length of 5-mm (⅕-in) wide metal chain between the two eyes. This should be long enough to allow the lids to stay open without falling shut.

Mitre the moulding for the front panel *(7 and 8)*, and fix it with panel pins and glue along the guidelines. Make sure it is squarely set, using a set square. Paint the dressing table with a coat of primer. Allow this to dry, and then apply a top coat of gloss paint. If you want the front panel to give the illusion of being a pair of drawers, you can screw two handles to the front panel.

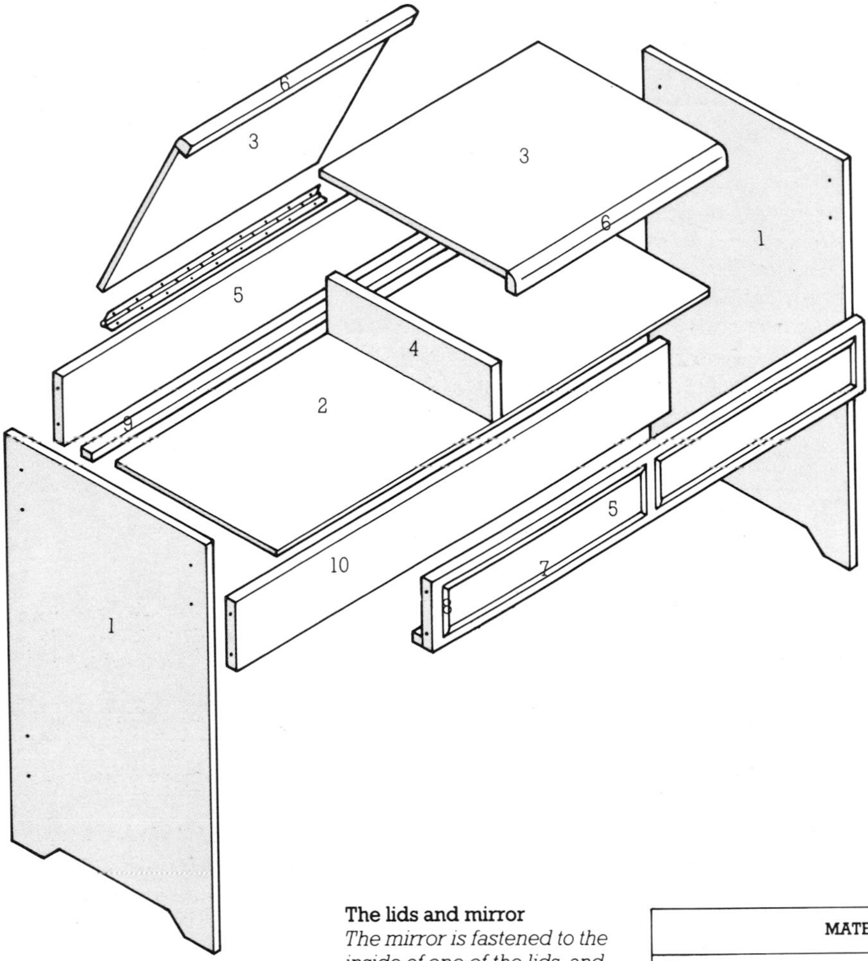

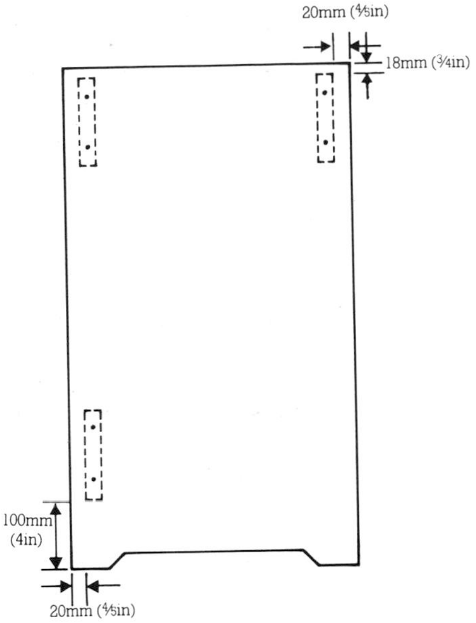

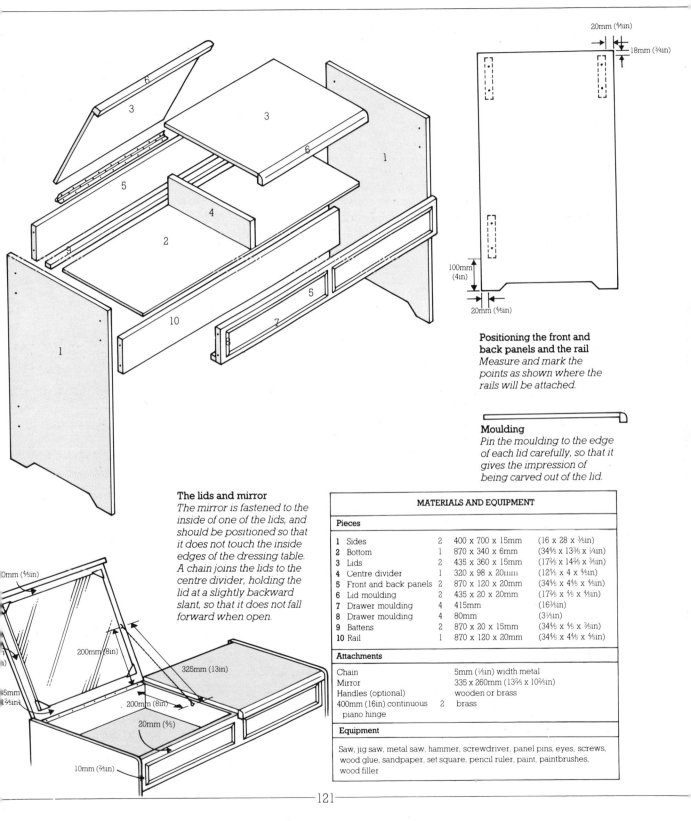

Positioning the front and back panels and the rail
Measure and mark the points as shown where the rails will be attached.

Moulding
Pin the moulding to the edge of each lid carefully, so that it gives the impression of being carved out of the lid.

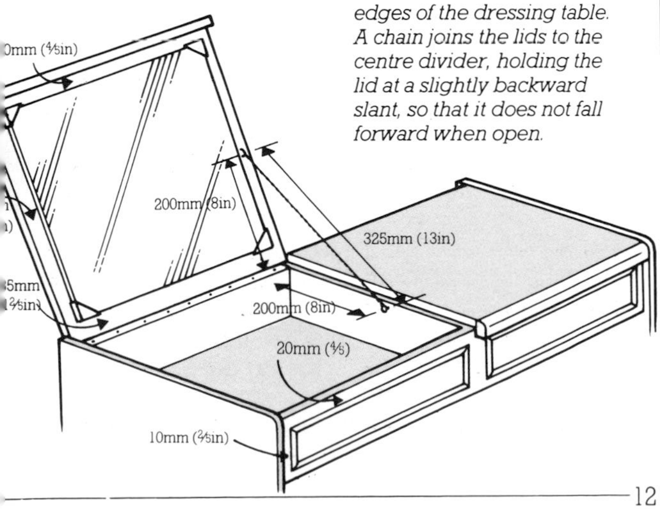

The lids and mirror
The mirror is fastened to the inside of one of the lids, and should be positioned so that it does not touch the inside edges of the dressing table. A chain joins the lids to the centre divider, holding the lid at a slightly backward slant, so that it does not fall forward when open.

MATERIALS AND EQUIPMENT

Pieces

1	Sides	2	400 x 700 x 15mm	(16 x 28 x 3/5in)
2	Bottom	1	870 x 340 x 6mm	(34 4/5 x 13 3/5 x 1/4in)
3	Lids	2	435 x 360 x 15mm	(17 2/5 x 14 2/5 x 3/5in)
4	Centre divider	1	320 x 98 x 20mm	(12 4/5 x 4 x 4/5in)
5	Front and back panels	2	870 x 120 x 20mm	(34 4/5 x 4 4/5 x 4/5in)
6	Lid moulding	2	435 x 20 x 20mm	(17 2/5 x 4/5 x 4/5in)
7	Drawer moulding	4	415mm	(16 3/5in)
8	Drawer moulding	4	80mm	(3 1/5in)
9	Battens	2	870 x 20 x 15mm	(34 4/5 x 4/5 x 3/5in)
10	Rail	1	870 x 120 x 20mm	(34 4/5 x 4 4/5 x 4/5in)

Attachments

Chain		5mm (1/5in) width metal
Mirror		335 x 260mm (13 2/5 x 10 2/5in)
Handles (optional)		wooden or brass
400mm (16in) continuous piano hinge	2	brass

Equipment

Saw, jig saw, metal saw, hammer, screwdriver, panel pins, eyes, screws, wood glue, sandpaper, set square, pencil ruler, paint, paintbrushes, wood filler

SPACE SOLVER

As children take that dramatic step into the teens, most parents face a space problem. Not only do clothes, stereos, books and other possessions take up more and more room – this is the age of the group, in which teenagers often sit for hours in their rooms with their friends, talking endlessly, listening to music and drinking cup after cup of coffee! Here, the problem is tackled at source by getting rid of the biggest space consumer – the conventional bed – and fitting a folding bed as a replacement.

What you should do is to disguise the bed. This way, it becomes an integral part of the decorative scheme, not a sore thumb. You could, as here, install a fitted cupboard next to the bed, in which you can store bedlinen when it is not in use, and cover the front of it with the same paint and wallpaper as the rest of the room. Decorate the space revealed when the bed is let down in a complementary colour that will look warm and attractive, and fit an overhead light into the recess for reading in bed. This system has been designed so that the shelves revolve on a pivot, and the ornaments and books on them do not have to be removed at night.

Rag-rolling
Give rather plain pieces of furniture a sense of unity by painting them in the same colours. Here, the desk and rocking chair were both rag-rolled and then painted with a floral motif that was inspired by the design of the wallpaper.

Following through
Always follow a design theme for a room through to its logical conclusion. The panels on the desk and the door are accentuated by the introduction of a second, striped, wallpaper, itself set in a panel on the wall. The striped paper also serves as an effective background for the two paintings, which would lose their impact if hung against the floral wallpaper.

Hiding doors
You can disguise a fitted wardrobe by treating it as part of the wall, and papering it to match the rest of the room.

Saving space
The bookshelf unit rotates through 180°, to reveal the bed recessed at the back. A locking mechanism holds the unit in place so that it stands firm when in use as either a bookcase or a bed.

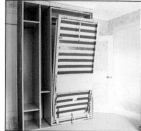

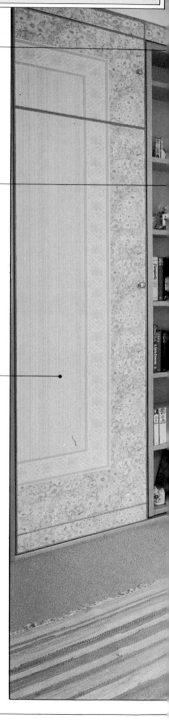

GENERAL HINTS

Once you have decorated a room, you will want to keep it looking its best. You will be able to do this by careful cleaning, and periodically checking the furniture for damage.

Touching up paintwork

It is inevitable that, over the years, any furniture you have painted will become scratched or chipped; this will be especially the case if you have young children, who are bound to be careless.

To touch up paintwork successfully, firstly you must try to match the original colour as closely as possible. Unless the furniture was painted with one solid colour, and you can remember the name of the manufacturer and the shade, you may have to blend several shades of paint together to get a match. Make sure that the paint is also the same finish – gloss or matt – as the existing paintwork.

Once you have the right colour and finish, dab a small artists' brush into a little of the paint. Drop tiny globules of paint into each scratch mark. Do not stroke it on – the paint will fill the scratch much better if it is dropped into it. If the scratch is so large that it is a gouge, you will have to fill the hole first with proprietary filler, allow it to dry, and sand it down. Then carefully paint the filler with undercoat, and drop the paint on to the surface.

Protecting decorations

By varnishing decorations such as stencils, *trompe l'oeils* and murals once you have finished painting them, you will find that you will save yourself a lot of work. This will also make them much easier to clean, and protect them from dirt and scratches.

A varnished mural or stencil can be gently cleaned with a damp cloth and a little washing-up liquid. You can remove stubborn marks, such as those caused by felt-tip or ball-point pens, with a damp cloth and a small amount of household cleaner.

Looking after wood

Keep any wooden furniture or fittings you have in good condition by polishing them regularly. Make sure the coats of polish do not build up and become sticky by always rubbing the polish well into the wood, so that it feels smooth to the touch, and not tacky.

Protect your furniture against woodworm by checking it occasionally for the tell-tale signs of small holes. Woodworm will only spread if not treated in good time, and you can do this using a proprietary woodworm killer. If you are unsure about this, or have discovered woodworm in a valuable piece of furniture, seek the advice of an expert.

Cleaning soft furnishings

Loose covers can either be dry-cleaned or washed, so if you have covered a piece of furniture yourself, you should have taken note of the cleaning instructions. You will find loose covers and cushion covers easiest to remove if you have fitted them with zips

Any spills should be mopped up as soon as they occur, and then treated according to the substance that has been spilled. If you have to dampen a fabric and scrub it clean, be careful not to make the material too wet. Otherwise, the water may soak through to the stuffing, and will cause some foam fillings to disintegrate. Always read the manufacturer's instructions if using a proprietary dry-cleaner, as it may harm some fabrics and fillings. When removing a stain, always work neatly from the outside in, otherwise you will spread it, or leave a ring.

Curtains can be periodically taken down and washed or dry-cleaned, or you can clean them in situ. You will find this easiest if you use a special vacuum cleaner attachment.

Caring for floor-coverings

You will spend more time cleaning these than

any other part of your house. If you allow the dirt to build up in a floor-covering this will be difficult to remove when you do clean it.

Carpets and rugs should be vacuumed or cleaned with a carpet sweeper. You can shampoo them yourself, using a proprietary carpet cleaner, but do allow this to dry fully before you replace the furniture. Otherwise, the fibres of the carpet or rug will be flattened, and any metal casters on furniture will leave rusty patches on the wet carpet. Avoid showing any balding patches of well-worn carpet. Move the furniture around from time to time to even out the wear on the carpet.

Cork tiling should have been sealed with a protective coat of polyurethane or varnish when it was laid. It should be swept to remove surface dirt and dust, and then cleaned with a damp cloth or mop. Persistent grease marks can be removed with a very little white spirit. Sealed wooden floorboards should be treated in the same way.

Never polish a floor so hard that it becomes dangerous, especially if you have young children, and don't polish areas of floor that are usually covered with rugs, or these will slip. You want a clean floor – not a skating rink!

Cleaning walls

Painted walls can be washed. Brush them first to remove any dust or cobwebs, then wash them using warm soapy water. Wring out the cloth as dry as possible, then work in a circular motion, moving from the bottom to the top of the wall, so the water doesn't drip. Then, working from the top of the wall down, go over the area with a cloth wrung out in clean water. You will find it easiest to clean small areas of the wall at a time, overlapping them slightly.

Many wallpapers are washable, in which case you should follow the manufacturer's instructions, having first brushed the wall or cleaned it with a special vacuum cleaner attachment. When you wash the wallpaper, make sure it does not become too wet. Otherwise the paper may pucker when it dries, and the wallpaper paste may become weakened.

STAIN AND REMOVER	CLEANING METHOD
Clear and contact glue – *acetone, or amyl acetate* **Latex glue** – *dry-cleaner* **Ball-point and felt-tip pen** – *methylated spirit* **Crayon** – *dry-cleaner* **Grass, leaves and flowers** – *glycerine or methylated spirit* **Plasticine** - *dry-cleaner* **Grease, butter, cream, oil and tar** – *dry-cleaner* **Pencil** – *rub out first with an eraser then use dry-cleaner*	*Scrape off any excess you can with a spatula or knife. Test the cleaner first on a small inconspicuous piece of the material you are cleaning to make sure it does not harm or discolour it. If possible, lay the material wrong side upmost, and then put a cotton pad underneath the stain. Apply a little of the recommended cleaner, working from the outside of the stain inwards. Blot dry. Repeat if necessary. When treating carpets with a dry cleaner, check the manufacturer's instructions first. Some dry-cleaners may damage the backing of the carpet.*
Blood and egg – *cold water for fresh stains, enzyme detergent for dried stains* **Fruit, fruit juices and jam** – *borax solution, peroxide or carpet shampoo* **Milk** – *lukewarm water for fresh stains, borax solution or carpet shampoo for dried stains* **Urine** – *enzyme detergent or carpet shampoo* **Vomit and faeces** – *absorbent material, then enzyme detergent or carpet shampoo*	*Soak up any excess with an absorbent material. Use sawdust for solid surfaces, and french chalk for fabrics.* *Wash washable fabrics in an enzyme detergent. Never soak wool, silk, and non-colour-fast fabrics.* *Try sponging stains on non-washable fabrics with cold water. If this does not work, sponge with the lather of an enzyme detergent.* *For carpets and upholstery, use a proprietary shampoo, or a stain remover for small spots. Sponge the stain remover on gently. Do not soak the fabric or carpet with shampoo. Rinse by sponging with cold water. Try to air the fabric or carpet afterwards so that it can dry properly.*
Heat marks	*To remove these from wood, rub with brass cleaner, working along the grain. Then repolish the wood.*

INDEX

Copyright and copying

If you want to make an exact copy of an existing design – from a book or a magazine, say – you should check whether or not the design is copyright in advance with its publishers. This advice particularly applies if you want to have the design photocopied and scaled up or down. Most publishers are normally happy to give such permission, provided that your design is not for commercial use.

Acknowledgements

The publishers and the author would like to thank the following for all the help they have given: Laura Ashley Ltd, 49 Temperley Road, London SW12; C Brewer & Sons Ltd, Decorators, 327 Putney Bridge Road, London, SW12; and Sally Miles, who did the spacescape mural and the mouse house mural.